SCARRED
BUT
UNSCATHED

GROWING IN FAITH

To Dottie –
Thank you for your
purchase. I hope something
herein resonates with you.
God bless.

Peace
Jennifer
3/9/21

JENNIFER G. SNEED, PH.D.

Published by Mindstir Media, LLC
45 Lafayette Rd | Suite 181| North Hampton, NH 03862 | USA
1.800.767.0531 | www.mindstirmedia.com

Cover Designer: Wesley Hall/Illustrator@thebrowngram

Printed in the United States of America

ISBN-13: 978-1-7363845-4-1

DEDICATION

This book is dedicated to my parents – the late Reverend and Mrs. Leo (Annie) Sneed – who not only taught me about faith but about how to live life with faith in Jesus Christ as your anchor. It is also dedicated to my Macedonia Baptist Church family, without whom the book would not have been possible.

ACKNOWLEDGEMENTS

Toni Morrison said, "If there's a book that you want to read, but it hasn't been written yet, then you must write it."

This book is the result of many years of consternation and some years of work to bring it into being. Through it all, one person has been there to encourage me, support the writing when it felt like slogging through the mire, and to tell me, "You can do this!" That person is my husband, Scott, who has the patience of a saint. If I needed to adjust my schedule, he was all for it. When I would work until 4:00 a.m., he let me sleep and brought me tea when I awoke. I know this journey was not mine alone, and I cannot tell him how much his ongoing love and support have meant to me.

Then how can I even begin to acknowledge the many roles that my Macedonia Baptist Church family, the leadership of the Reverend Leonard D. Comithier, Jr. Institute ("the Institute"), and Reverend Comithier have played in the development and writing of this book. From the beginning of the project ("The Macedonia Book Project") through its completion, individual members have listened, cajoled, shared, and supported me in ways that I am not sure they are even aware of. The leadership of the Institute expressed their concern for my health as I undertook this project but gave me their whole-hearted support. Pastor Comithier, without hesitation, provided his full support of the project and later, in response to my surprise request, willingly allowed me to interview him for a story. It is just so clear, based on this process, that the "Macedonia experience" is a real thing and I am grateful for it.

I would be truly remiss if I did not acknowledge the inspiration, guidance, and support provided by my friend, Dr. Gretchel Hathaway. Little did she know that when she began nudging me to "get that book finished" that I was almost at a standstill. She devoted hours to reviewing chapters, helping me organize my thoughts, and listening to me lament about the slowness of my progress. For all the time and work she gave to me and this project, I am forever in her debt.

I know that I have acknowledged my Macedonia church family, but I must separately and especially thank the eighteen people who volunteered to share their "transformative faith experience(s)" with me. Without these volunteers, this book could not have been written. This group of people was kind and patient as the months and years passed. They allowed me to poke and prod with my lists of questions into their lives. They shared their stories freely. I thank each of them for their willingness and their trust. I definitely could not have done it without each of them.

One of the key strategies to improve your work is to have others review it and give you feedback. I deeply thank each of the reviewers – Rev. Dr. Michael B. Brown, Dr. Tamika Carey, Sharon Cates-Williams, Jennifer Coplin, Louis Coplin, Rev. Dr. Angela Davis, Rev. Kara Dunn, Sandra Herndon, Debora Brown-Johnson, Jacqueline Lake-Sample, Elsa Magee, Dr. Janice Pride-Boone, Rev. Chaun Richardson, Dr. Betty Shadrick, Sandra Stuart, and Dr. Jonathan Wright. Your feedback was instrumental in improving the quality of the manuscript. Your time and thought have been priceless to me.

And then there is my editor, Dr. Susan Perkins of ColPerResearch Inc. We were introduced by a mutual friend who told me Dr. Perkins, or Susan as I came to call her, was a "really good" editor and that she had been very pleased with her services. It is not easy to lay your work before someone else to critique. Susan graciously guided me through cleaning up my manuscript and expanding it where needed, while keeping me centered with the greater power of God working through her. She is indeed a powerhouse and I am forever grateful to her for taking me on.

Finally, I thank God, my source of strength, power, and peace, who has guided me in writing *Scarred but Unscathed: Growing in Faith*. At this point, I can say without a doubt that He has much for me yet to do and I will fearlessly continue on my faith journey. To God be the glory.

Endorsements

"*Scarred But Unscathed*" is an amazing narrative of faith, unseen in action throughout the life of Dr. Jennifer Sneed and those persons she interviewed. The transparency detailed in these stories is awe inspiring and filled with unwavering faith, hope, and inspiration. Dr. Sneed's approach to this writing is brave, honest, and reflects the many measures of faith that exist through out the body of Christ.

Rev. Dr. Angela A. West
Former Associate Minister, Macedonia Baptist Church

An informative and thoughtful collection of testimonies, Dr. Jennifer Sneed's *Scarred But Unscathed: Growing in Faith*, underscores the importance of continually tracing God's presence and hand in our lives. Written with grace and sophistication, *Scarred But Unscathed* reminds us that even if God allows us to experience hurt *sometimes*, God *always* enables us to overcome.

Tamika L. Carey, Ph.D.
Author, *Getting to Know Him: Observations and Experience From My Walk of Faith*

If you have never had your faith tested, reading the life stories in *Scarred But Unscathed: Growing in Faith* will certainly give you a good idea of what it means to have faith in times of adversity. This is a book that you will read more than once.

Sandria Stuart
Former Member Macedonia Baptist Church
Trusted Friend

Many people do not fully grasp that faith is progressive. Our faith grows over time through our life experiences. Kudos to Dr. Sneed for being transparent enough to let people know that her faith was tested and grew through tough circumstances. Stories like the ones she tells in *Scarred But Unscathed: Growing in Faith* give people hope that they can make it through their tough times to something better.

Rev. Chaun Richardson
Associate Minister, Macedonia Baptist Church

The book was an easy and thoughtful read. The stories matched the title... *Scarred But Unscathed: Growing in Faith*. I teared up just thinking about the power of God and how He always brings us through the toughest of situations. The scriptures are artistically woven around the author's story reminding the reader of how we are all inextricably connected through our experiences. A great book for Bible class or a workshop on faith and God's love.

Debora Brown-Johnson
Subject of Chapter entitled "Unwavering"
Deacon, Macedonia Baptist Church

"*Scarred but Unscathed: Growing in Faith* is balm for the soul. The personal stories of tests, coping, and faith are palatable and lifegiving. Dr. Sneed's story and her guests' stories show us all how to get through painful and difficult times. I strongly recommend the book for any one that believes in faith, hope, and purpose."

Rev. Kara N. Dunn, M.Ed., M.Div.
Founder and Pastor of Joy Springs Ministries

Dr. Sneed's wisdom of sharing her traumatic story while including others' spiritual experiences allows for the reader to relate to and embrace their own triumphs and challenges. For each story, you are taken into that person's most challenging life experiences as you walk with them through their journey in a prayerful manner. You feel God's presence as you begin to relate to the incidents as they strengthen your own views of faith and purpose. You will want everyone you know to read this book and discuss the stories of how a spiritual setting will enhance your belief in life ever after.

Dr. Gretchel Hathaway
Vice President of Diversity, Equity and Inclusion, Franklin and Marshall College
Author of *A Bonded Friendship: Moses and Eliphalet*

Jennifer Sneed is an educator, writer, thought leader, and a woman of deep personal faith. In *Scarred But Unscathed*, all those qualities come together to make a fascinating read.

Dr. Sneed shares with the reader her own experience of suffering, chronicling the faith and courage required for her to break free from a dangerous cycle and make the journey to healing and wholeness. Having thus identified with the individuals she interviewed for this book, she proceeds to present their stories in captivating fashion — stories of people who believed that God can make a way when there seems to be no way. And one-by-one, their faith was proven true.

This is a can't-put-down book that can bring inspiration to a single reader or can serve as a stimulating study resource for a small group. Either way, I recommend it wholeheartedly.

Dr. Michael B. Brown
Former Senior Minister of Marble Collegiate Church, NY, NY
Creator and Presenter of 5 Steps to a Loving and Purposeful Life, PBS

Table of Contents

ACKNOWLEDGEMENTS 5

ENDORSEMENTS 8

FOREWORD 13

INTRODUCTION 15

Part I: Growing and Strengthening Faith . . . 25

Chapter 1: Church – My Community of Faith. 26

Chapter 2: In the Beginning 35

Chapter 3: Living Life 45

Chapter 4: More 52

Chapter 5: Wilderness Experiences 55

Chapter 6: The Power of Prayer 62

Chapter 7: Without a Question 69

Part II: How Deep Is Your Faith?. 75

Chapter 8: How Deep is Your Faith? 76

Chapter 9: Peace be Still 99

Chapter 10: In His Way 112

Chapter 11: Rooted 116

Chapter 12: Stronger Now. 122

Chapter 13: Overcome Evil with Good. 127

Chapter 14: Help 137

Chapter 15: Here for a Reason 145

Chapter 16: A Full House 154

Part III: Walk On By Faith 159

Chapter 17: Walk on by Faith 160

Chapter 18: Just Leave It. 164

Chapter 19: Determined. 169

Chapter 20: Death Changes You 175

Chapter 21: Unwavering. 181

Chapter 22: But by God's Grace 187

Chapter 23: Building Bridges 199

Chapter 24: Faith in Freefall 206

CLOSING REFLECTIONS 215

EXERCISES TO GROW YOUR FAITH 219

FOREWORD

My spiritual sister, Jennifer Sneed, Ph.D., provides for us in this book what is more than merely personal anecdotes or inspiring essays. She unpacks before us considerable wisdom. **Scarred but Unscathed** creates a picture which affirms both the eternality of life coupled with the interrelatedness of all lives.

In these times of unrestrained divisive spirits, it is heartening to be beckoned to a place where my transformative experiences can resonate with others in a different time and space. That is the supreme test of our destiny.

Dr. Sneed has taken the liberty entrusted her by God and those who have shared her faith journey to bear witness to the truth that we are all "caught up in a network of mutuality, clothed in a single garment of mutuality."

If what has been written in these pages will cause a deeper reflection into where you and I have been and are going, how we are being encouraged, and how our ongoing experiences with life will be enhanced and shared, Dr. Sneed, this work will have been well worth the effort.

"...whatsoever things are true, whatever things are honest, whatsoever things are just, whatsoever things are pure, whatsoever things are lovely, whatsoever things are of good report; if there be any virtue, and if there be any praise, think on these things." Philippians 4:8

Reverend Leonard D. Comithier, Jr.
Pastor, Macedonia Baptist Church
Albany, New York
Author of *More Than Sunday Morning*

INTRODUCTION

"Now faith is the substance of things hoped for, the evidence of things not seen." (Hebrews 11:1 KJV) This is the definition of faith that I grew up with. My father, who was a Baptist minister, quoted it often during his sermons over the years. Faith. The word has served as a cornerstone for not only my life, but the lives of countless others. One would not think a short word of five letters could cause such debate about its meaning. Some of the debate about its meanings stems from determining the basis for its definition.

Faith is often viewed as the property of those who are religious, whether within or outside of an organized denomination. A religious faith hinges on belief or trust in God or a set of operational principles for one's life. If someone belongs to a specific denomination, for example, Baptist, Catholic, Methodist, Jewish, Muslim, Buddhism, Hindu, etc., that denomination outlines a set of beliefs or principles by which to live. Those principles are often based upon the writings of a specific deity, saint, or other identified leader or founder of the denomination.

However, faith can be simply based on the ideas or conclusions one has come to hold dear, such as a belief that good things happen when a certain color or item of clothing is present. Some people have faith in a lucky charm like a rabbit's foot or in unique circumstances such as odd- or even-numbered days of the month. Others are equally adamant that faith does not exist at all, and they believe those who express faith in anything are wasting their time and energy.

The notion of faith has been an undercurrent throughout my life, and the question of how that came to be begs for an explanation. Was I born believing in God and holding certain basic principles sacrosanct? Was I indoctrinated, as some people might want to believe, and unable to discern or separate my beliefs from those of the community in which I existed? What is the language to even begin a discussion of faith on a personal level?

Although the subject of much research and many books, there is no single definitive explanation of how one moves from not having faith to having faith or vice versa, or from having faith through others to having faith from within yourself. In his book, *Stages of Faith*, James W. Fowler refers to the work of H. Reinhold Niebuhr and Paul Tillich, who posited that "faith...is a universal human concern...."[1] Fowler went on to add that "...whether we become nonbelievers, agnostics or atheists, we are concerned with how to put our lives together and with what will make life worth living...."[2] Although I have been part of an organized religious community all of my life (actually since birth because my parents were deeply rooted in the Baptist church and I joined church by the time I was eight), I never had to sit down and pen what faith meant to me or how I came to have it. It was always something acknowledged by my elders, something I learned to describe according to the tenets of, in my case, the Baptist Church Covenant, the Bible, Sunday School, and other church school materials, as well as my parents.

I recall being so excited on the day of my baptism. I was probably seven years old. Our church did not have a baptismal pool so we would go to Miller Park, a local park, and use the lake. On my baptism day, there was a long procession of cars carrying families to the park to witness my immersion into the waters

---

1   Stages of Faith by James W. Fowler, HarperOne, 1981, p.5.

2   Ibid. p. 5.

of the lake and my emergence as a new Christian in Christ. My friends and schoolmates who attended my church usually viewed a baptism as a great opportunity to go to the park and knew after the baptism there would be food and time to play. The adults seemed to be in a much more somber and serious mood regarding baptism. They carried a certain air of solemnity and deep appreciation of the ritual and its underlying beliefs.

I remember being wrapped in sheets and towels to stay warm, as I only had a thin layer of clothing on in anticipation of the baptism as we rode to the park that Sunday before the sun reached high noon. (The sheets and towels also kept me warm after the baptism when my mother and other church ladies wrapped me in them as they walked me to a place to change out of the wet clothes.) My father, the pastor, was going to baptize me just as I had watched him baptize many others. Since I was short, he had to locate a rock to put in the water in the spot for me to stand on as he pronounced the tenets of baptism. He spoke of John baptizing Jesus in the Jordan River being like being baptized in the lake and recounted from the Bible that this baptism is with water, but God baptizes with the Holy Ghost. The last thing I heard was, "I baptize you today Jennifer in the name of the Father, the Son, and the Holy Ghost!"

Even though you think you won't be surprised when the water rushes across your body and then surges over your face as you are plunged backwards into the lake, when it actually happens you are not at all ready and it does not feel the way you imagined. You blink, gasp, swallow what to a child seems like gallons of water, and are lifted back up in one flowing and continuous slow motion. You reach to wipe the water draining off your head and face, blink quickly in an attempt to clear your vision, and suddenly you hear it: the clapping and voices saying "Amen!" and "Hallelujah!" and the congregation beginning to sing "Amen, amen, amen, amen, amen, amen." You feel the joy as it emanates from those watching from the shore and moves like a wave toward you. When that joy reaches you, it almost physically lifts you from the water and provides a comfort like you have never before felt. Even as a young child, I knew something unlike anything else, something inexplicable had happened to me.

That was the beginning of my faith walk. Not that I would have had the wherewithal to call it that at the time. In fact, it would be many years before I would use that nomenclature to talk about the spiritual side of my life. What I could use and did use in the intervening years to frame what faith was for me were the models of faith exhibited by my parents, the stories shared in Sunday School books, and, as I grew into young adulthood, lyrics from gospel and spiritual songs and hymns, like:

▸ My faith looks up to thee; Thou lamb of Calvary, Savior divine! Now hear me while I pray, take all my guilt away, O let me from this day be wholly Thine![3]

▸ When peace like a river attendeth my way, when sorrow like sea billows roll. Whatever my lot, thou hast taught me to say, 'It is well, it is well, with my soul.'[4]

▸ My hope is built on nothing less than Jesus' blood and righteousness; I dare not trust the sweetest frame, but wholly lean on Jesus' name.[5]

▸ We have come this far by faith, leaning on the Lord; Trusting in His holy word, he's never failed me yet.[6]

---

3   *"My Faith Looks Up to Thee."* Words by Ray Palmer. Music by Lowell Mason.

4   *"It Is Well With My Soul."* Words by Horatio G. Spafford. Music by Philip P. Bliss

5   *"The Solid Rock."* Words by Edward Mote. Music by William B. Bradbury.

6   *"We've Come This Far by Faith."* Words and Music by Albert A. Goodson. Arranged by Thurston G Frazier. Copyright 1965.

- In times like these you need a Savior; in times like these you need an anchor; be very sure, be very sure your anchor holds and grips the solid rock! This rock is Jesus. Yes, he's the only one. This rock is Jesus, the only one! Be very sure, be very sure your anchor holds and grips the solid rock![7]

And Bible verses, such as:

- "Now faith is the substance of things hoped for, the evidence of things not seen." (Hebrews 11:1 King James Version – KJV)
- "They are new every morning; great is thy faithfulness." (Lamentations 3:23 KJV)
- "And Jesus said unto them, Because of your unbelief: for verily I say unto you, if you have faith as a grain of mustard seed, ye shall say unto this mountain, remove hence to yonder place; and it shall remove; and nothing shall be impossible unto you." (Matthew 17:20 KJV)
- "His lord said unto him, Well done, thou good and faithful servant: thou hast been faithful over a few things, I will make thee ruler over many things: enter thou into the joy of thy lord." (Matthew 25:21 KJV)
- "If then God so clothe the grass, which is to day in the field, and tomorrow is cast into the oven; how much more will he clothe you, O ye of little faith?" (Luke 12:28 KJV)
- "And now abideth faith, hope, charity, these three; but the greatest of these is charity." (1 Corinthians 13:13 KJV)
- But the fruit of the Spirit is love, joy, peace, longsuffering, gentleness, goodness, faith." (Galatians 5:22 KJV)

I can look retrospectively and reflectively now and clearly see how faith grew in me over the years. It was not a straight

---

7   *"In Times Like These."* Words and Music by Ruth Caye Jones. Copyright 1944; 1972.

trajectory by any means, but overcoming each challenge and surviving each obstacle enhanced my belief that I was not in this thing called life alone.

This book did not start out as what you are about to read. I had what I thought was an incredible idea. An idea I had been sitting on for probably fifteen years, an idea that I felt needed to be brought to life, but I had multiple excuses, along with a bit of fear, for pushing it (more like shoving it) behind anything – somewhere out of sight.

I have survived sixteen surgeries (none of them elective), two rough marriages, single parenthood coupled with an intensely full career, and in 2002 a horrendous accident (you will learn more about that later). I know there is a divine message in my survival. I know others have lived through situations and experiences that have strengthened or altered their spiritual or faith journey, and that their stories also need to be told. Something inside me always said I would be the portal through which others can tell their stories...to usher them into the world so that people beyond our immediate church community can benefit.

I was not sure how to make this book come to life. It was to be a book of transformative faith experiences – mine and others that, in retrospect, reflected how God's hand has guided our lives. One night as I sat at home contemplating how to celebrate my birthday, I was struck with the thought that the stories I was going to help birth resided in people all around me, and especially at my church, the Macedonia Baptist Church ("Macedonia") of Albany, New York. I have been a member of Macedonia for almost thirty years. I raised my daughter in the church. I have sung in the Gospel Choir ever since joining, and my closest friends are members of the congregation. The pastor, Reverend Leonard D. Comithier, Jr., has grown to not only be my pastor but a trusted friend. Somehow, I needed to be able to reach out and invite members to share their stories with me.

A month prior to my sixty-fifth birthday, an age demarcated by our society as becoming a "senior," I had an epiphany. The church was in the midst of expanding its initiatives to address issues relative to education, leadership and professional development, job readiness, and other areas. I wanted to give back to the church and the community, and heaven knows, I love a challenging project. Why not make it a church project? Then the "how" question returned. The revelation came to me to make it a project whereby members could volunteer to share their stories through interviews with me, and I would incorporate them into a book, along with my own story.

I developed a project proposal to share with the leaders of the Reverend Leonard D. Comithier, Jr., Institute ("the Institute"), part of the Macedonia Baptist Church created in 2016 to provide information, training, support, and advocacy, as well as to host relevant programs sponsored by other organizations. The leaders of the Institute supported the project, and I was scheduled to present the project to the congregation on the Sunday following my birthday – October 15, 2017. I prayed that someone would want to share his or her story with me. The time came and the presentations seemed to go off without a hitch. Deep breath!! It has been said that everyone has a story. Before I could get out of church that day, several people stopped me to let me know they had stories to share. Then I looked in the box I had left in the vestibule to collect sign-up slips...it already had twelve slips in it!

Within the pages of this book I will share my story, along with the stories shared with me by eighteen people, including Reverend Comithier. As you read these stories, you will notice that some contain multitudes of facts that can be corroborated or verified through research, i.e., checking newspaper stories, investigating town histories in local libraries, and digging through public health records. However, given that this is a book of faith stories, the reader must have some degree of trust that those who shared their experiences, insights, and lives were sharing from the depths of their souls, and that they were in communion with a spirit greater than themselves, with no desire to bend the truth. It is my hope that each reader will find stories that resonate with his or her life and experiences.

Volunteers were offered the choice of using their real names or choosing a pseudonym – not an insignificant decision when your story will be in print and shared with people you do not know and are unlikely to meet. Everyone's story is personal, and it can be unnerving to place it in the public's eye. Although most interviewees ultimately decided to use their given names, some had uniquely private reasons to select a pseudonym. Either way, all interviewees acknowledged that their story reflected significant developments in their faith journey.

At this point I should also declare that this book is not being written to argue about the existence of God or to determine the penultimate definition of faith. I do not claim to be a Bible scholar or theologian. I am a preacher's kid and have lived in the community of faith all my life, even before I could speak. I have observed churchgoers – members and non-members, church dynamics, operation, and etiquette in the Black church. I have taken in hundreds of sermons by numerous preachers – some pastors and some not. I have attended and participated in many church events and activities including "ministries" and "auxiliaries." I am not a preacher, but I cannot promise not to include a biblical reference here and there.

This book is divided into three parts: Part I: Growing and Strengthening Faith, Part II: How Deep is Your Faith?, and Part III: Walk on by Faith. Each part begins with a segment of my life's experiences followed by stories of those interviewed. The stories reflect the diversity of situations experienced and paths taken by those interviewed and share insights gained from conquering addiction to surviving a life-threatening attack. In some cases, it is evident that the experience transcends the reality that we are familiar with and required me, and hopefully you, to look beyond what is in the physical realm to what may be in the spiritual realm. You may have to dispense with pure logic and put on the lens of a voyager on a trip to an uncharted region.

Scarred but Unscathed: Growing in Faith concludes with "Exercises to Grow Your Faith." Feel free to peek at the exercises prior to finishing the book to jumpstart your thoughts regarding how these stories might inform your choices and decisions going forward.

PART I:
GROWING AND STRENGTHENING FAITH

CHAPTER 1:

Church –
My Community of Faith

"Train up a child in the way he should go:
and when he is old, he will not depart from it."
(Proverbs 22:6)

Initially I thought my story was fairly common in that I was the product of a two-parent family, raised with two older brothers in a relatively close-knit community in Bloomington, Illinois. The community centered on the church my father pastored at the time. Our home would be considered a happy one, even though by today's standards we lived in the "low socioeconomic" band... not in poverty but not in the middle class. I only learned this when I entered college and took a sociology course. Prior to that time, all I knew was that most people in our community lived similarly. We lived in a small, two-bedroom church parsonage during my grade-school years. My two brothers slept in one bedroom and my parents in the other. I had a twin bed in the dining room. The house was kept "white-glove-test" clean. My mother was a stickler for cleanliness and organization. If the fumes from Clorox, Pine Sol, and Lysol did not make your nose hairs curl, it just was not clean. Our family never went hungry. In fact, it seemed to me that we had an abundance of food.

Between my mother and the church ladies, our refrigerator-freezer and cabinets were always full. I do not remember worrying about clothes or whether they were clean. The only clothing concerns revolved around whether we had the right dress clothes for church. Given that stipulation, somehow, we always had new clothes for whatever the special occasion happened to be – Christmas, Easter, and pastor's anniversary being the pinnacle events of our year. It was not until years later, after living much more of life, that I would discover that the experiences of my life were unique and could perhaps be used to help others make their way through difficult or challenging situations.

I can basically say I grew up in church and be factually correct. I can also say I grew up around preachers, in particular Black Baptist preachers. My father, grandfather on my mother's side, uncle, and great uncles on my father's side and, at this point, several cousins are preachers. Preachers were always at our house, especially on Monday mornings to discuss what had happened at their churches on Sunday and to share the highlights of their sermons. In fact, at a young age I learned how to make coffee in a percolator to serve to the preachers who came by on Monday mornings.

As far back as I can remember, I was in church for a service or program. My life was filled by Sunday School, 11:00 a.m. worship service, 6:00 p.m. Baptist Training Union, choir rehearsals (for my mother and then for me), Missionary Society and Mother's Board meetings with my mother, Easter/Christmas/Mother's Day/ Father's Day/Children's Day programs, weddings, and funerals. At times when no one else was home to watch me, I had to go to the church with my dad while he counseled church or community members or attended to various tasks. Church was where I had my first experiences with technology – mimeograph machines, duplicating machines, and electric typewriters. Church is where

I learned to play the piano and organ, as well as to design a printed program. Church is where I learned to speak in front of a crowd.

One story occurred early in my father's ministerial journey. I do not know whether I actually remember the incident or whether I have heard it so many times over the years that it has become part of the collective consciousness of our family. My father was preaching at the Progressive Baptist Church in Chicago, Illinois. The church was large enough to have a balcony where my mother sat with me and my two brothers. Being the youngest, around four at the time, it was the perfect place from which to see my father at the pulpit preaching one of many sermons as he trained to one day become an ordained minister and later a pastor. The members of the congregation were "filled with the Spirit" with some waving their hands in the air, some nodding their heads, some fanning themselves with their funeral-home fans – a staple of the Black Baptist church. Even as a four-year-old I could tell something exciting was happening. With all the gusto a four-year-old could muster, in a clear and sufficiently loud enough to draw attention voice, I said, "Amen, Daddy!" According to my mother, this was quite the talk of the members after the service. Even then, without the ability to articulate any of it, I felt love surrounding me. Church was my second home, and that was fine with me.

Throughout my life I have found the church environment to be filled by warmth, acceptance, and a feeling of security and love. That environment has kept me afloat through a myriad of traumas and work situations that were not remotely reflective of those characteristics. Over the years I began to lovingly refer to my community of faith and its people as "my tribe" – a reference borrowed from sociology but modified. French sociologist Michel Maffesoli coined the term "urban tribes" to describe small groups of people defined by shared interests and lifestyle preferences around which modern societies are organized.[8]   My tribe supported me as a single parent and through moving from one location to another. My tribe has included my pastor and church family, a smattering of non-church friends, advisors, mentors, and consolers (when needed).

My father began his ministerial journey by attending the Moody Bible Institute, a theological seminary in Chicago, Illinois. He was ordained as a minister under the tutelage of Reverend Retha Brown at the Progressive Baptist Church, also in Chicago. My father became a Baptist pastor when I was six years old. One of his favorite sayings was, "Don't worry. God will take care of it!" This would often annoy my well-organized mother, who planned in advance for just about everything, but who could argue with that belief? My mother's grandfather was a Methodist minister and, although I don't know much about him or remember him, I do know that my mother grew up in church and, as an adult, practiced her faith on a daily basis. She never let us forget that God is who we should go to in prayer, and that we are not "the end all be all," meaning do not get too full of yourself.

The faith that my parents lived by was evident in how they addressed the challenges of life, and there were many. I grew up in the '50s, '60s, and '70s. Racial prejudice and discrimination; employment and housing inequities; blocked voter registration and voting; and segregated, ill-equipped schools were the norm and not the exception. Just prior to my starting 1st grade, our family moved from Chicago to a predominately White small city called Bloomington-Normal, Illinois. The hyphenated name reflected that Bloomington and Normal were separate small cities that jointly

---

8   Lovene, Frank. 2014. "Sociologist: Descartes Created The Crisis of Modernity and "Urban Tribes" Will Fix It." Business Insider. https://www. businessinsider.com/afp-urban-tribes-thriving-in-modern-society-2014-10?utm_source=copy-link&utm_medium=referral&utm_content=topbar.

capitalized on several of the area's attributes. The community boasted of having two universities, being a national center for corn production, and being home to major candy and dog food companies. My father became the pastor of one of the town's three major African-American churches at the time. My brothers and I suddenly became the "preacher's kids." I was immediately struck by how others deferred to him and the respect bestowed upon him. I was so proud to be the preacher's kid, but at the time I did not understand exactly what it meant. The more the role of "preacher's kid" unfolded, the more I was certain that it was not going to be any fun. I watched my mother become the "first lady" of the church. She was a young woman who was beautiful, articulate, and naïve. Little did she know what a "first lady" had to contend with, in terms of attitudes and expectations from the congregants of the church. This was my introduction to watching my mother ask God to give her strength. Over the years, she asked God for other things as well, such as patience, healing, and greater faith.

In his sermons, my father often used the biblical definition of faith – "the substance of things hoped for, the evidence of things not seen" (Hebrews 11:1 KJV). My parents had great faith. Their faith got us through hard financial times, illnesses, racial prejudice, misbehaving and often misguided children, and a long list of other issues and ailments. Growing up in this environment, it was almost impossible for me not to have some sort of spiritual awareness to help me navigate life and all that it entailed. This is not to say that I was always in perfect communion with God or that I did not go through troubling and rebellious teen years, questioning young adult years, or hard-headed adult years. However, I knew in my heart that God was real and that any time I fully surrendered to Him everything would work out just as my father always said – "God will take care of it."

The church community, as with any community, has weathered its share of controversy and been disrobed under the microscope. Looking at recent history, some church leaders have been charged with, and often been found guilty of, behaving egregiously in relation to congregants in terms of behaving sexually inappropriately and misallocating funds. Some of the more infamous scandals include televangelists such as Jim Bakker,[9] who allegedly committed sexual assault along with bilking his congregants out of $158 million. Then Ted Haggard[10] and Bob Coy[11] were charged with allegedly engaging in gay sex and child molestation. Jimmy Swaggart[12] was allegedly involved in pornography. Probably the most notorious breach of acceptable behavior of men in religious leadership positions was evidence of sex crimes against children committed by Catholic priests and covered up by church leaders, bishops, and cardinals for many years. In addition to leaders not abiding by the trust invested in them by their members and communities, some churches,

9   https://abcnews.go.com/US/scandals-brought-bakkers-uss-famous-televangelists/story?id=60389342
https://allthatsinteresting.com/pastors-behaving-badly#9
https://www.washingtonpost.com/archive/lifestyle/1989/08/29/jim-bakker-driven-by-money-or-miracles/525a2b1b-95c7-447a-980a-e81b2357d36a/?utm_term=.6f12bf9c3fd3
https://popculture.com/tv-shows/2017/09/28/jessica-hahn-sex-scandal-jim-bakker-ptl-club/#2

10   https://allthatsinteresting.com/pastors-behaving-badly#9
http://www.cnn.com/2009/US/01/29/lkl.ted.haggard/

11   https://www.christianpost.com/news/megachurch-founder-bob-coy-accused-of-molesting-4-y-o-sexually-abusing-her-into-her-teens.html
https://en.wikipedia.org/wiki/Bob_Coy

12   https://allthatsinteresting.com/pastors-behaving-badly#8
https://en.wikipedia.org/wiki/Jimmy_Swaggart
https://www.cnn.com/2012/06/11/us/gallery/pastor-scandals/index.html

such as the Crystal Cathedral built in Orange County, California, allegedly used funds contributed by hardworking people who lived modestly to build structures that dwarfed surrounding neighborhoods and reflected a focus on "consumerism and not [spiritual] transformation."[13]

Clearly the church is not perfect. People bring their human-ness with them when they become a member of the clergy or any community of faith. Through the 24/7 news cycles and social media, people are now exposed to every indiscretion of the church and every image that reflects the failings of organized religion. Such was the case when I was growing up, but to a lesser degree or a less publicized extent. There is no intent to minimize the seriousness of the failings of church leaders or the effects of their misbehaviors on their victims or their congregants. However, I learned over the years that the situations highlighted in the news represent a small percentage of the millions of people involved in religious organizations and communities. Even given the many newsworthy transgressions of members of the church, I have watched those in my tribe continue to live in a way that reflected deep spiritual beliefs.

Faith in a divine spirit is the basis of the Christian church community, and whether that divine spirit is referred to as God, Jehovah, Yahweh, Abba, or another name is irrelevant. The fact that there is a Christian belief system that weaves the fundamental elements of faith, hope, and charity (I Corinthians 13:13), as well as the commandment that we love one another (John 13:34-35), into the fabric of the community is the sustaining characteristic. Those elements – faith, hope, charity (love) – are the ties that bind together the individuals within a community to support one

---

13 http://www.christiannewswire.com/index.php
 https://en.wikipedia.org/wiki/Christ_Cathedral_(Garden_Grove,_CA)

another through good times and bad. Evidence of the existence of the community is both visible in the interactions among the people of a church and felt by other individuals when in the midst of their members.

Why bring the concept of "community of faith" to the forefront early in this book? As you read the stories contained herein, you will notice some commonalities that I ignore at this point but instead prefer to see where the stories take you. You will come to understand why I say Macedonia, my community of faith, has received God's blessings because it has been generous beyond its walls – food to those without, support for those experiencing life's challenges, and an uplifting, relatable message to those who are receptive. Just as with the churches located in Macedonia, Greece at biblical times, "Moreover, brethren, we do you to wit of the grace of God bestowed on the churches of Macedonia" (2 Corinthians 8:1 KJV).[14]

As we age, many of us come to certain realizations and understandings as we become retrospective about our lives and reflect on our journey. During our young adult years, we are often focused on surviving the daily grind of work and raising children, the intoxicating and seemingly freeing effects of addictive substances, the physical and emotional demands of recovery, the sting of racism, or the other traumas life presents. There is often little, if any, connection to a deeper meaning of the events, circumstances, and situations of life.

Contributors share their stories with the understanding they are now able to bring to their lives; they believe their stories might be helpful to others. Each person contemplated deeply to pull from his or her life's collection of experiences those things

---

14 https://www.biblegateway.com/resources/commentaries/IVP-NT/2Cor/ Macedonian-Believers-Model

that most strongly impacted their development as a person and contributed to their definition of faith. After all, whether our life experiences move us to become Christians, "...nonbelievers, agnostics, or atheists, we are concerned with how to put our lives together and with what will make life worth living."[15]

The people in this book, including me, have come through a myriad of life situations and circumstances. Each person may not have been able to articulate how they processed each event or how they viewed each event at the time, but the common theme is that they continued moving forward with their lives. They did not give up when faced with what seemed like insurmountable odds. Each story contains events the individual navigated or survived but, in many cases, the word faith would not have entered into the description of the process. Some people did not connect their arrival at a new point in life or their survival to any spiritual or religious beliefs. Some people, due to their connection to organized religion or their religious practice, found an inner strength that they later named faith. The more that inner strength demonstrated its power, the more they believed in it – the more they believed in the source of their strength. For yet others, it might have been years before the seeds of a spiritual belief system took root and yielded a distinct ideology around faith. However, retrospectively, they realized that there was nothing they could have done that would make God reject them, even when they rejected themselves.

The words you will come to be familiar with are retrospection and reflection. Anchor those words in your mind as you read about the situations encountered and paths traveled by me and eighteen others.

---

15 Stages of Faith – The Psychology of Human Development and the Quest for Meaning. James W. Fowler. Published by HarperOne, 1981. Pg. 5.

CHAPTER 2:

In the Beginning

"Now faith is the substance of things hoped for,
the evidence of things not seen."
(Hebrews 11:1 KJV)

Each person within a church community of faith experiences that community differently. Therefore, what is contained within these pages is not necessarily generalizable to the population at large. Although, given how the worldview of many has changed since the 2020 advent of the COVID-19 global pandemic, the words that follow may be more poignant than ever. The stories provide a small window into the psyche of nineteen people who, looking back, can undeniably say they did not get through life's experiences and challenges on their own. I am no exception, and here is my story.

Life. Some people say, "It's what happens while we're waiting." Waiting for any number of different things at different points in our lives. Waiting to be old enough to drive, graduate, or finish a project. Waiting for our money to be balanced to move, purchase a specific item such as a car, house, or vacation, or have children. Waiting to find the right partner, job, or neighborhood. We tend to have an idea of what we want to obtain and sometimes of what we want to happen. We may have the best plans and intentions to achieve our dreams, but there are times when those plans and intentions just do not work, regardless of how much we want them. Langston Hughes asked the question, "What happens to a dream deferred?"[16] The follow-up question I pose is how do you deal with the challenges or impediments that interfere with obtaining or achieving that which you have dreamt of? Do you become bitter and cynical? Do you enter a phase of denial and pretend nothing happened? Do you recover, review, and move forward? Which approach do you take as life continues and over which we have little control? Perhaps it is not fair to expect that we would respond the same way at each point in our lives. After all, a five-year-old might stomp off if he or she does not get to go play, but let us hope that same person would not respond the same way at age thirty-two.

Like others, I too had plans as I matured...plans to go to college and then graduate school, get married at some point, have a family and live the American dream with the house, car, and vacations. That was *my* plan. Little did I know that, even as young as age five, not only had I already veered from the ideal, but that my life path would take me through many life-altering situations. Looking back, it is clear events that happen in our lives can be used to push us to either be better human beings... or not. If you subscribe to a spiritual tradition, it can push you to live to a higher standard...a standard that incorporates love, faith, and the desire to share your beliefs with others. As I look back, I wonder how the events that occurred when I was young, unaware of possible consequences and incapable of making

---

16 *"Harlem"* (also called *"A Dream Deferred"*) poem by Langston Hughes published in 1951 as part of <u>Montage of a Dream Deferred</u>.

informed decisions, contributed to how I determined my approach to serious situations and events later in my life and how the early events shaped my faith beliefs.

I was born in Chicago, Illinois, and, like most people, I do not remember my earliest years except through stories shared by my family. Somewhere around the age of four, it became apparent that I needed to have my tonsils removed. The only detail I recall was the horrendous smell of ether gas, used at the time to sedate patients prior to surgery, and the joy of being able to eat unlimited (or so it seemed) amounts of ice cream afterwards. Little did I or my family know that the tonsillectomy was the beginning of a long line of physical challenges on my path.

Within a year after recuperating from my tonsillectomy, my oldest brother, who is seven years my senior, was heading to the store. For what, I do not know. I know I wanted to go with him, but my mother had forbidden me to do so. I slipped out of our family's apartment and decided to tag along, unbeknownst to him. At five, I pulled off a covert operation. From my brother's recounting of the day, I apparently stayed far enough behind him that he was unaware of my presence. The route to the store involved crossing a busy street...this was the south side of Chicago. My brother crossed the street. In trying to keep up, I darted into traffic from between two parked cars and was immediately struck by a car. My other brother, who is two years my senior, recalls being told that the impact of the car was strong enough to toss my five-year-old body into the air. My mother shared that I was unconscious for three days and medical personnel were unsure whether I would survive. I recall none of this major life event.

Many say my survival was purely the result of medical technology, the skills of the physicians, and the amazing ability of the human body to recover. From my current perspective, I agree that medical technology and physician skills were important, but I believe there was a significant web of prayers that sustained me. Those prayers were based on faith in a power greater than us. Those prayers came from my parents and from the community of faith of which we were a part...Progressive Baptist Church.

James Fowler describes this age, five years old, as part of the Mythic-Literal stage of faith development.[17] Children of this age are unable to grasp concepts in theoretical form, so their "faith" is constructed from what they see and hear in stories shared with them by their parents, other significant adults, and members of their faith community (whether religious or non-religious). So, seeing and hearing my parents and others pray made prayer a critical element in the story of what was occurring in my life at the time. That was faith for a five-year-old.

Most physicians will tell you that they can only go so far. They cannot guarantee survival or healing. Beyond surgical skill, they say the rest is beyond their abilities to control. That is the space where faith and love come in. Can I say without a doubt that it was the faith expressed through prayers and love of my family and faith community that brought me through that accident? Is there empirical proof? Would I be alive if those prayers and that love had not been present? The Stanford Encyclopedia of Philosophy defines faith as something that "goes beyond what is ordinarily reasonable, in the sense that it involves accepting what cannot be established as true through proper exercise of our naturally

---

17 *"James Fowler's Stages of Faith,"* from his book <u>Stages of Faith – The Psychology of Human Development and the Quest for Meaning</u>, p.113. Also found at <u>www.psychologycharts.com/james-fowler-stages-of-faith.html</u>

endowed human cognitive facilities – and this may be held to be an essential feature of faith..."[18] Given the circumstances, my survival could have been considered something beyond what was ordinarily reasonable to hope for, but those who had faith and prayed believed that my little body would survive. These are questions that no one can definitively answer, and that this book will not attempt to answer. Hopefully, these pages will, however, raise questions to provoke your thoughts about your life's events and how you survived, failed, or thrived through them.

Shortly after surviving being hit by the car, my family had to move to the small college town of Bloomington, Illinois, because my father was called to pastor his first church. We suddenly went from being apartment dwellers to living in a house...the church parsonage! To a six-year-old, as long as I was with my family it did not matter, but for the first time in my life, we had a front and back yard. When we arrived at the house, the grass was tall. I could run through it and almost be hidden. The house sat on the corner at the top of a hill. On both sides the streets sloped downhill so skating, sledding, "race car" driving (built from boards, spare parts, and whatever we found), and just running as fast as you could consumed much of our time.

An old, unusable garage sat at the back edge of the property. Many of its floorboards had long since disappeared and those that remained often broke as soon as you stepped on them. Various remnants of workbenches and leftover cans of paint and oil rested against the walls. Most of the windows were gone and those that were not were so dirty you could barely see through them. Probably the most intriguing part of the backyard was the well. Coming from the city, I had never seen a well and this one was especially

---

18 Stanford Encyclopedia of Philosophy. First published June 23, 2010; substantive revision March 30, 2016. https://plato.stanford.edu/entries/faith/

fascinating because we – the kids – were not supposed to go near it. The well's opening was covered by large pieces of wood with very big rocks sitting on top. I do not know whether the well was natural or man-made, but its opening looked like a concrete block that rose about a foot above the ground. When the boards and large rocks were removed, we could see water through the three-foot-square opening which appeared to be about four or five feet below. Even when the well was open and sunlight poured in, the water glimmered black. We learned that the well was no longer used and that it was unsafe to play anywhere near it. My brother and I availed ourselves of every opportunity to remove the rocks and wood pieces to look in, drop things in, and fish anything out of that well. In addition, it became one of the main daredevil spots for kids in the neighborhood. The kids would dare each other to do various stunts like leaning into the well to pull a bug out or see who could lay on the ground and hold their head down into the well the longest. From my perspective, life was good!

Our elementary school was kitty-corner from the parsonage, so our home became the school stopping point and the drop-off point for many children from families who attended the church. I loved the company and we would watch *Captain Kangaroo* (a daily children's television series) until the very last minute; it ended at 9:00 a.m. when we were due in our classrooms. We would, at 9:00 a.m., make a beeline across the street to school. However, we were usually a few minutes tardy. This practice became so problematic that the school's principal had a talk with my parents to convey the importance of all the children making it to their classrooms on time for the first bell of the school day. Needless to say, we were in our seats on time following that talk.

I excelled in school and enjoyed reading just about any book available. When I was around eight or nine years old, my teacher noticed me struggling to make words out on the page and on the board. As a result, my mother took me to the eye clinic. After the various vision assessments, it was determined that I had strabismus, which meant that my eyes were not looking at the same thing at the same time. The muscles that controlled each eye were not working together and would need to be re-sectioned (either shortened or attached to a different spot on the eyeball) to avoid me ultimately being cross-eyed. I ended up having two separate surgeries over several months, requiring me to wear an eye patch after each one as part of the healing process. Although I do not remember being teased by other children, I do recall being called a pirate by my brother who was two years my senior. The corrective surgeries worked well, and I did not require further treatments – which was common as children matured. Again, things were good, and life continued with church, school, and community involvement.

At ten years old, my mother said I was limping. She could not figure out why and I complained that my left hip hurt. Off to the doctor. X-rays were taken from just about every possible angle. The scans were evaluated and the diagnosis: slipped capital femoral epiphysis, or SCFE. A SCFE meant the head or ball of the hip bone had slipped from the neck of the hip bone, resulting in pain, stiffness, limited motion, and limping. Once diagnosed, a child was no longer allowed to bear weight on that leg or the condition could worsen. So, immediately, there was no more activity for me; walking or running was out of the picture. Surgery was scheduled and a pin, that looked more like a screw, was inserted to hold the head of the bone on the top of my hip. Surgery, wheelchair for three months, crutches for two months, and physical therapy to learn to walk again consumed my 5th grade school year. I turned eleven years old while confined to the wheelchair. I had a homebound teacher that the school district was required to provide due to the length of my recuperation. The teacher came to our house several times each week to provide a few hours of instruction so that I would not fall behind educationally. Since our house sat on the corner across from my elementary school, I could see the children playing on the playground before school and during recess. I wanted so much to run and play. Some of my friends would stop by either before or after school to visit. I looked forward to those visits to find out what was happening during my absence but would become sad when my friends could march out the door and cross the street while I could not.

At eleven years old I did not consider myself to be disabled. I simply thought of the whole process of surgery, wheelchair, and crutches to be a temporary challenge. My memory brings forward images of me in the wheelchair racing around the house – much to my mother's dismay. I recall learning to do a wheelie to get up a slight step between the front door of the parsonage and the front porch. This particular skill was also not one of my mother's favorites for fear I would get hurt. I never did. I became rather indignant when I thought someone felt sorry for me. The only real issue, from my perspective, was negotiating stairs to get in and out of buildings. Handicapped accessibility had not yet become a law, and buildings often did not have any way for someone in a wheelchair to gain entrance or to exit other than being carried. I became extremely embarrassed and self-conscious when I had to be lifted, either with or without my wheelchair, into or out of a building – especially church! My parents prayed regularly for my healing. They were grateful and expressed their thanks to God for bringing me and our family through the surgery and healing.

Just prior to turning eleven years old, at the start of 6th grade I started limping again and experiencing pain in my right hip. Back to the doctor. Repeat the whole process again. Now the diagnosis changed to *bilateral* slipped capital femoral epiphysis. Even though there are theories, the medical community cannot definitively explain why SCFEs occur. The second time around made me miss my friends even more since I had not been back in school very long after the first hip surgery. My homebound teacher during this round really pushed me academically and believed I had exceptional abilities. Although the academic challenges distracted me from focusing on what I was unable to do physically, time could not pass fast enough for me. The six months until I could return to school seemed like an eternity.

Both pins were removed when I was sixteen years old, as was the practice at the time. Fortunately, that surgery (to remove both pins during one operation) did not require an extensive recovery process and I moved on with my high school life.

From a young child's perspective of the world, I was only aware of what was happening to me and how I felt. At the time, I could not even begin to comprehend what my parents were going through. What brought them through their youngest child being hit by a car, having her tonsils removed at a young age, two eye surgeries, and three hip surgeries all before the age of seventeen? I grew up observing how they lived and the faith they had that God would take care of everything. Their faith was strong. They did not question the existence of a power greater than themselves. So, even though I had not personally developed a deep spiritual life before my teen years, it was the prayers and beliefs of my parents and our community of faith that guided and supported me. As I moved into my mid-teens, prior to the removal of the pins, I had developed a greater understanding of the core tenets of the Baptist faith (salvation through faith, scripture as the foundational guide to living, and the representational power of baptism and the Lord's Supper) and adopted the practices of those in our family's community of faith (regular church attendance and prayer, participation in church life through auxiliaries or ministries, financial support of the church to the degree possible by a teenager). I used my parents and other church leaders as my models and felt comfortable in my place in the community. Fowler calls this the Synthetic-Conventional stage of faith development,[19] and it is a stage at which many people often remain throughout their lives.

---

19 *"James Fowler's Stages of Faith,"* from his book <u>Stages of Faith – The Psychology of Human Development and the Quest for Meaning</u>, p.113. Also found at <u>www.psychologycharts.com/james-fowler-stages-of-faith.html</u>

CHAPTER 3:

Living Life

"The Lord also will be a refuge for the oppressed,
a refuge in times of trouble."
(Psalms 9:9 KJV)

People often have chapters in their lives that they would rather forget. Chapters where you are not quite sure how to process the events that occurred or how to place that period into the context of who you were at the time or, later, who you have become. From a retrospective perspective, however, one often gets greater clarity. The period for me was my late twenties/early thirties. College was an exciting time. I met and interacted with people quite different from me, read voraciously, and engaged in discussions about esoteric topics such as the ethics of euthanasia and the morality or immorality of man. I did not take a break between undergraduate and graduate school and graduated without a hiccup. Academics were clearly my strong suit.

My first professional job marked another step toward full adulthood. The job was forty miles away in Peoria, Illinois, and required that I commute by car each day about forty-five minutes each way. When it became too much, I found an apartment in Peoria. The job was short-lived, as upward mobility in the organization was limited and the separation from family and friends became tedious. A year later I was searching for another job. By this time, my father pastored a church in Indianapolis, Indiana. I broadened my search to include Indianapolis and found a position there with the Indiana Vocational Technical College.

As a young adult, relationships were not one of my areas of strength. In Indianapolis, I dated as an individual and as part of groups of friends. There were good dates and ones that were not so good. Like most people as they experience life, my heart was broken a few times as I made my way through life's adventures. Then one day I met someone who seemed to check the boxes outlined throughout my life – he went to church, graduated from college, came from a decent family, had a healthy lifestyle, didn't drink, was gainfully employed, and was a preacher's son! We went out and found we had much in common. He made me feel attractive and desirable. We dated and enjoyed our time together. We enjoyed comparing our upbringings and sharing preacher's kid tales. He and his brothers enjoyed sports and physical challenges that resembled military-style obstacle courses. Their interactions were often some type of competition to determine who would "win." It all seemed perfectly normal for them. The details of this relationship were written in a journal I discovered as I cleaned out a closet.

My twenty-eight-year-old self was in love and was willing to unconditionally accept all parts of the guy who seemed perfect... almost. In retrospect, there were signs from the onset that I either ignored or decided reflected misgivings that were tolerable. As I re-read my journal, it was clear that by my late twenties, I had moved from relying on the faith of my parents to having what James A. Fowler refers to as "Individuative-Reflective" faith,[20] a faith foundation of my own based on having been exposed to the world outside of my immediate family and church environment.

20 Fowler, pp. 174-183

I had left home, been to college, met people who lived very differently, moved to two different cities, and assumed financial responsibility for myself. All of these life experiences gave me the opportunity to discover that others' spiritual, religious, and faith beliefs were not the same as mine, but that did not necessarily mean they were less valid. It also gave me the opportunity to begin to figure out just what I believed separate from my parents, church elders, and faith community practices.

As I moved into this relationship with Stephen, a man I ultimately married, I would ask God to "give me strength and understanding" or note that "praying definitely makes a difference." Yet my human side, my youthful naivete, was not willing to accept that many of the characteristics displayed by this man of my dreams were inconvertibly abusive. In August 1981, about three months after being engaged, I wrote that I would "have to pray for guidance to let God redirect his negative energies into other things," while admitting that "his temper still scares me." Over the course of three and a half years, this relationship teetered between real lows of verbal and physical abuse and exhilarating highs of enjoying Stephen and our friends, a little traveling, and reuniting after being separated by distance for extended periods of time. As I ended one journal entry on April 25, 1982, my faith was evident as I "thank[ed] God for giving me strength, the fortitude and the courage" to remain in the relationship, although looking back, that strength, fortitude, and courage were misplaced. The wedding date was set for December 24, 1982. I was thirty years old, brimming with excitement at the prospect of being married, but at the same time I was "still concerned to a smaller degree about his temper." At two weeks prior to the wedding, my journal entry read, "I've prayed about it and I know God will take care of it/me/both" – referring to the relationship, me, and my then-fiancée.

The wedding date came. The two families and some friends came together in my parents' living room for the ceremony, followed by an intimate reception. It is hard for weddings to be anything but lovely. It was. Life moved on, although it seemed at a rather slow pace. We returned to Ithaca, New York, where I had taken a teaching position in September that year and Stephen was enrolled in a master's degree program in psychology at Cornell University. Upstate New York weather was cold and bleak, which did not contribute toward making anything seem bright and cheery. We fought a lot from the start of the marriage – usually triggered by accusations of my failing to inform him of any overspending, wanting to have friends over, or small things like bread pieces not cleaned from the sink quickly enough. During one fight, I was choked to the point of unconsciousness. On February 10, 1983, I wrote, "I was just praying that I wasn't killed before the end of the month. I have never been so petrified in my entire life. I was scared to the extent that I put a bag of 'get-away things' together and put them in a place I could always get to." By day, I was a respected school administrator, but during nights and weekends, I became a timid, reclusive person that I did not even recognize.

"I pray[ed] regularly..." Throughout the relationship, and subsequent marriage, I had faith. On July 28, 1983, I wrote, "I'm sure that God has a reason for us going through this process. Sometimes I think it is to help us realize that we are not the directors of our fate. We are His and He determines what we will or will not do. It is His way of instilling within us His law of obedience. Without Him we can do nothing. So, we wait upon the Lord; pray and be patient." We rented a small house in Ithaca, and I discovered that potting flowers and having lovely colors around me during the summer brought me a modicum of joy and comfort. In the fall, I continued working in the school district as a special education administrator and teacher. Prayer was my anchor. In the spring of 1984, I found out that I was pregnant, which both excited me and caused me some degree of anxiety as I contemplated raising a child in the unstable environment in which I lived. By the time the school year ended, being guided through prayer, I had made the decision to leave the marriage.

Making the decision meant I had to figure out how to leave, which was tricky given how closely my husband watched my schedule in terms of when I came or left the house, and how performing certain duties routinely seemed to keep the peace in the house...at least it seemed that way. Since the end of the school year meant I would have a month or so off work, it gave me more flexibility than I had during the school year. I decided to make a reservation to fly home (to Indianapolis where my parents lived) without telling my husband, and I planned that I would leave the house while he was away from the house, either on campus or participating in an activity related to his martial arts group.

The day came, and I went through the usual activities – breakfast, washing the dishes, and straightening up the house, as in making the bed and making sure the living room and kitchen looked orderly. Stephen went about his regular activities. I could hear and feel my heart pounding in my chest, knowing that I had to quickly pack as soon as he left the house. I had already gone through my list of clothes and other necessities to pack in my mind so it would not take me long to get them out and put them in a bag. Being four months pregnant did not slow me down. I had gone to the bank the previous day to withdraw some cash. I also made arrangements for my best girl friend to take me to the airport, so I called to let her know it was clear to come pick me up. I told her that I was not certain when I would return. In my mind, though, I knew I would be back in time for the start of school in the fall. She questioned how long I thought it would be before Stephen discovered I had left not just the house, but the town. I told her typically he would be out at least a couple of hours, and when he arrived home, he would think I had gone to the store without leaving a note...about which he would be upset. It would be about four hours before he might suspect something was awry, but by then I would be well on my way. We were both nervous, though, until the plane lifted off the runway.

I felt every muscle in my body relax as the airplane climbed higher and higher into the sky. I wondered what other people's stories were on the flight and whether they were also running away from something. I thought about the baby growing in my womb and how I was doing this not only for me but for him or her (did not know the gender at this point). Releasing the tension allowed me to doze off into a sweet slumber. It seemed as soon as I did, however, the plane was landing in Binghamton, New York, and my name was being called over the public address system. I was to check in with the flight attendant. As I took this information in, my mind scrambled to determine why I would need to identify myself to the flight attendant. I timidly raised my hand and the attendant came directly to me. She told me that the captain needed to speak with me! I was both perplexed and nervous that the captain of an airplane needed to talk to me. As soon as the plane landed, the captain came to my seat to tell me that there was an emergency and that my husband had called the airport to speak with me. The pilot escorted me, the pregnant woman, off the plane and into the airport to a telephone in an office area. My hand shook as I took the receiver. Stephen had figured out that I was headed to Indianapolis and which flight I had taken. He asked what I thought I was doing, and I responded, "Leaving you!"

This caused him to become irate and he screamed that I should get the next flight back to Ithaca. I told him I had no intention of doing that and hung up. The captain saw that I had ended the conversation and had someone escort me back on the plane. The escort could see that I was upset so offered me some water once back on the plane. My heartbeat roared in my ears until the plane was lifting off toward Indianapolis. I knew Stephen would not be there when I arrived. I took a deep breath, closed my eyelids, and prayed that my parents would be at the airport when my plane landed. They were. As I exited the secure area, they embraced me in a way that was reminiscent of being in a safe, warm cocoon. I felt their love and acceptance engulf me. They did not know what had transpired during my married time in Ithaca, and I never told them all the details. However, because we were close, they knew whatever had occurred had to be incredibly serious for me to return home without explanation. I remained in Indianapolis for the summer of 1984 and returned to Ithaca in time for the start of school that fall. By that time, Stephen had returned to Indianapolis to live near his family. My daughter, Simone, was born November 9th – healthy and happy.

Reading my journal at this point in my life, I wonder how I stayed so long and why. The courtship and marriage, as all parts of one's life, were part of my faith growth and development. This chapter of my journey was completely between God and me. I had shared details with my best friend, but because of fear and shame, no one else. Faith gave me the fortitude and resilience to survive and thrive through a dark time.

CHAPTER 4:

More

*"Be careful for nothing: but in every thing by prayer and supplication
with thanksgiving let your requests be made known unto God."
(Philippians 4:6 KJV)*

I entered the 1990s as a single, working mother. I felt a certain psychological lightness being physically liberated from the abusive marriage, as well as feeling spiritually stronger knowing that I was not alone even though I was a single parent. I was comfortably into my third position with the New York State Education Department working as a Supervisor of Research and Development in the Office of Special Education Services. The job was both challenging and exciting as we worked to develop and produce publications for schools and parents regarding special education. It was clear to me at this point in my life that every situation or predicament was temporary and would pass. I just had to use the gifts that God gave each of us to make decisions and plans, and to persevere through them.

The 1990s, however, did bring more physical challenges and surgeries. Surgery is not an uncommon phenomenon in our lives. Surgeries are performed every day and night. Some are considered "routine," while others are considered "a matter of life and death." However, at the most fundamental level, surgeons can neither guarantee success nor promise that there will be no complications. Even they acknowledge that at a certain point, the outcome is out of their hands.

On the way home from an office holiday party, while riding as the backseat passenger in a colleague's car, the car hit a patch of ice and slid into a tree. Everyone was more shaken up than seriously injured. The car sustained the most damage. As I got out of the car, my nose felt as if it had a headache. In an attempt to soothe it, I gently ran my fingers over it. Funny how one does not often feel one's nose. I was not sure whether it was injured, but it hurt. Everyone told me to go to the emergency room or an urgent care to have it checked and I reluctantly agreed. Once back to the parking lot where I had left my car, I drove to an urgent care center. Although I was not sure it was injured, the X-rays clearly indicated it was broken. As I explained to the doctor what had happened during the accident, we surmised that my nose had actually collided with my right knee at the point of the car colliding with the tree. The doctors were able to immediately schedule me into an outpatient surgery appointment to reset the bones. Again, I experienced God's grace in that the process of surgery, and healing did not result in sinus or other nasal problems over the long term.

Not long after recuperating from my broken nose, in performing a self-check, I noticed a lump in my left breast. Having read and heard much about breast cancer, finding the lump gave me pause. Your brain wants to go immediately to the end of the pier and jump into "oh my goodness, it's cancer!" I knew I could not go there. Even though I had found a lump, I was still responsible for caring for my daughter and going to work. Therefore, as difficult as it was, I had to remain calm until such time that a determination could be made regarding its condition. I prayed for peace and strength and made an appointment with my doctor. When the appointment time came, I was anxious for the examination. She confirmed what I felt and told me that most lumps are benign. The doctor tried to perform an aspiration, but the lump was hard. The needle could not penetrate it. An excisional breast biopsy was scheduled and performed about two weeks later. The lump was found to be benign. Amen.

In 1998, I was bleeding heavily each month. My doctor performed an ultrasound and found that I had large uterine fibroids. She described them as the size of apples and peaches but indicated that they are typically non-cancerous. These types of fibroids were not (and are not) atypical in African American women. After discussions with my doctor, surgery was scheduled and performed to remove my uterus and ovaries (full hysterectomy). My faith community supported me through the surgeries and subsequent recoveries, but by my late thirties I did not need to solely rely on the beneficence of others to appeal to a power greater than myself for strength and healing. The numerous physiological and psychological life events had given me a perspective about life and living that demonstrated the significance of faith. I could lift my own voice to the heavens, to God, while knowing that whatever the situation or event, it too would pass.

Just as my life's path took me through a variety of situations and events, so too do the life paths of May, Wysdom, and Sharon F. The following chapters share how the faith of three women grew to guide them as they traversed uncharted waters. Do they march forward without hesitation and doubt? Do they veer from the path onto detours, or are they confident about their options and decisions? No one knows where their lives will take them, not even May, Wysdom, and Sharon F.

CHAPTER 5:

Wilderness Experiences

"To the Lord our God belong mercies and forgivenesses,
though we have rebelled against him."
(Daniel 9:9 KJV)

May said, "You just might as well not even bother to think that you are not going to have to go through anything once you surrender yourself to God." She believes it's really kind of silly to think, "I've got this!" She knows everyone is still going to have to deal with situations and other things that get thrown at them during their lives. May calls these situations her "wilderness experiences."

May was born at home in a small town in Mississippi called Matherville about ten miles east of Shubuta with a population of less than 500 people. Since the town was very rural, May and her family did not get into town very often, but when they did, she recalls seeing "Whites Only" and "Colored" signs on restrooms and water fountains, as well as a segregated movie theater. May never went to school with White children. Her parents were sharecroppers. Her father, who was illiterate, had a great sense of humor, but he was a functional alcoholic who became abusive when he drank. Her mother had a 5th grade education but was extremely hardworking. May, her five sisters, and her parents worked in the fields. May remembers picking cotton, pulling corn, and stripping cane. The family did not make much money as sharecroppers. The White people who owned the land "kept the books" and let each family know how much money they had made at the end of each season. May said they were doing well to clear $300-400. Taking care of a family of eight on $300-400 was not an easy task. The girls had few store-bought dresses. Her mother bought material to have their clothes made by a female friend using money she earned by selling candy and working in White women's homes as a domestic. Her father was an avid hunter, and he would bring home rabbit, squirrel, deer, or other game meat. The family also kept a garden where they could grow fresh fruits and vegetables. At that time, a family had to be as self-sufficient as possible. May recalls never going hungry and always having clean clothes to wear.

Her first "wilderness experience" happened before she was old enough to fully understand or process the implications. May had grown up working in the fields alongside the rest of her family. Around the age of eleven or twelve, she was told to go work in the house to help the landowner's wife – a White woman – with housework. May found out that the wife was not home when she was assigned to go work in the house. May did not think much of it until one day the husband began touching her and trying to force her onto the bed. To May, the man seemed quite old. As she recounts the experience, she thinks he might have been in his late fifties or early sixties. He pushed her around, grabbed her private parts, and clearly intended to rape her. She later learned that he was incapable of consummating any sexual act. His inability, however, did not prevent him from tormenting and threatening May. She had heard from her mother and others that the man did not believe in God and had no compunction about behaving as he pleased with those in his employ. In his mind, May was there for his pleasure as he saw fit. May had to silently live with the fact that he had molested her. May did not tell her parents or anyone else about the incident that time or the next two or three times it occurred. She was afraid to tell her father, as he might confront the landowner and she knew that could lead to the Ku Klux Klan beating or killing him. So, she went about her field work and continued going to school.

Since no one talked about "it" – the sexual molestation and rape of Black women sharecroppers and their daughters – and those molested or raped received no counseling to deal with the trauma inflicted by the landowners and their sons, May did what hundreds of other women had done. She buried the memory and moved on with her life. Within the Black families in her immediate community, May said when she or any other young family member asked questions regarding sex or relationships, they were told that it was "grown folks' business" and that was the end of any discussion. Many families, at the time, had children who were fairer than the other children and had finer hair, and it was an unspoken fact that those children were fathered by a White male, usually a landowner.

The magnitude of the prominence of sexual molestation and rape of female Black sharecroppers and their families occurring during the 1940s to 1960s was not yet seen as a national crisis and would not be for years to come. One of the early cases (1947) would be that of Rosa Lee Ingram, a Black sharecropper sentenced to death for slaying, in self-defense, a White male sharecropper who lived on the same property as Ingram and her family and who sexually harassed her for years. Ingram's sentence was finally overturned in 1959 (McGuire, 2010). The case of Recy Taylor (1944), also a sharecropper, who was abducted, raped, and left on the side of the road, would also bring to light the impunity enjoyed by White men in the South during those years. The men who attacked Recy Taylor were never indicted and never forced to stand trial. It wasn't until the release of the book, *At the Dark End of the Street: Black Women, Rape and Resistance – a New History of the Civil Rights Movement from Rosa Parks to the Rise of Black Power* by historian Danielle L. McGuire that the Alabama Legislature offered Ms. Taylor an apology for its failure to prosecute her attackers ("Sharecropper who fought for justice after 1944 rape in Alabama," *The Irish Times*, Author Unknown, 2018).

May made a promise to herself that, as soon as she could, she was going to leave Matherville. She graduated from high school on May 22, 1966. By May 31st, May was gone. First, she landed in Chicago, but it was too big, too noisy, and too dirty. May was intimidated by the city, its size, and its rhythm. She knew she had relatives in upstate New York, so she talked with them. They invited her to come to Albany. She went. Albany had a different feeling about it... a certain familiarity. It felt "nice," like it could be home.

May married in 1967 and stayed married for seventeen years. She would classify many of those years as part of a "wilderness experience," as it was a period when she often drank, smoked marijuana, and briefly used crack cocaine. She admits that there were good times in the marriage, and her daughter is the product of those better times. May is most thankful for her daughter. It was clear, however, that her now-ex-husband was, as she calls him, a philanderer and that was made even more apparent when the accident happened. In 1973, she was five months pregnant with her daughter. She and her husband were deeply involved in selling cosmetics, trying to establish their own business. One evening they decided to go out with another couple that was also in the business. May cannot remember why, but the other woman was driving their car. All May remembers is that the friend driving did not maneuver the car back into the right lane when trying to pass another car. She knows the car rolled over three times, and because her leg was wedged between the seats, it was twisted and pulled out of the socket. She ended up having two surgeries while she was pregnant. She could not walk for the duration of her pregnancy or the eight months after the accident and the surgeries. During this time of needing support, the one person that she thought she could count on – her husband – was not available. That added to her pain. As May shared the experience, she could still feel the misery.

Throughout her adult life, May recalls being aware of a still, small voice in the back of her mind. During her young adult years, she thought it was her mother's voice, but as she matured, she thought it was the voice of God telling her she wasn't raised to behave or live as she was at the time. May knows she has not always been the woman she is now. She understands now that as she went through times of smoking reefer, using crack cocaine, drinking, and flirting, she was searching for something she could not articulate. She thinks it was the influence of her parents, especially her mother, that helped her not get mired in that life. She had a praying, church-going mother. During one of May's low periods in the late 1980s or early 1990s, she smoked marijuana that she later found was laced with an unknown drug. May could feel the effects of the marijuana but was not completely overtaken by it. As she laid in her bed, she heard loud voices but knew no one was around. A bright light shone, and a voice told her to "Put this mess down! This is not you!" She put the joint down and did not smoke again for years.

Even when she was smoking, May would pray to God to take the desire away. To deliver her from it. By the mid-1990s, May had found Macedonia Baptist Church in Albany. She met people there who made her feel welcomed and accepted. She worked in the kitchen to help prepare food. She sometimes went to the church to meet one woman in particular and they would talk as they cleaned bathrooms as part of their volunteering. She was not aware of it then, but that time was therapeutic for her. Often the women would pray with her. She kept going to church and over the course of three years, May became more spiritual and her faith became stronger. Ultimately, she joined the church. She remembers often going to visit the women deacons who lived in the house next door to the church, and just sitting on the porch talking about the issues life presented to her. She reached a point where she no longer wanted to participate in or be around those who did participate in getting high or using illicit substances.

May says it was not until she was almost fifty years old that she had a deeper understanding of what faith in God meant and how God works in one's life. She admits that although she was "brought up" in church, she was only in church in her younger years because her mother "made her" go. Now she understands that she had not internalized the true meaning of love and faith. Now she understands that through her faith she always has a connection with God and that she did not have to go through any of the hard times in her life alone. She understands that all of her misguided relationships, drug use, and drinking were attempts to anesthetize herself to fill a spiritual void that she did not recognize at the time. Now she reads the Bible and prays. She never went to a rehabilitation program to stop drinking or using drugs. She says your mind must be made up that you want to step away from that life. With her wilderness experiences behind her, May now says that when you are in that life, you are steadily looking for the feeling you had when you took your first puff or had your first high, but you never find it again no matter how much you indulge. May believes that "you go through what you go through for a purpose...to make you who you are!"

CHAPTER 6:

The Power of Prayer

"There is no fear in love; but perfect love casteth out fear because fear
hath torment. He that feareth is not made perfect in love."
(1 John 4:18 KJV)

When you think of wisdom, you often think of the ideas, thoughts, opinions, and actions that have been shared with you by someone you admire...someone who has overcome obstacles to reach a goal...someone who has demonstrated strong convictions by their actions and words...someone you may want to be like or emulate. The reality of wisdom, however, is that everyone has some degree of it, but they may not be aware of it until further down their life's path.

"You're a warrior, Mommy!" That is what her oldest daughter, who was around ten years old at the time, said. "You're a warrior." Wysdom had not taught her to use the word in that manner but was glad she saw things in that light. It was 2007. She and her two daughters were newly emancipated, for the second and last time, from a diseased marriage and family situation. She was struggling to put up a curtain rod to have some coverage over the windows of their new apartment before nightfall. She was not, by any means, a "handy" woman. She would use the heel of a shoe to hammer a nail or a butter knife as a screwdriver. She was a "frilly" female. But now it was just her and the girls, and she needed curtains at her window. She was determined to get them up. Her daughter saw that spirit in her, so Wysdom responded, "Yes, I am. I am a warrior!" Knowing that her daughters viewed her as a warrior gave her fuel to continue and not give up. She knew, and wanted to ensure her daughters knew, they were all going to be just fine.

Wysdom originally married her husband in 1996 as a young, twenty-six-year-old woman. Unlike many young women, though, she had no storybook images of love and marriage. Marriage for her was a way to have a stable life and to provide a foundation for having children and raising a family. She did not enter the proposition with the romanticized, movie version of the starry-eyed damsel seeking her knight in shining armor to rescue her. She sought a man who was kind and dependable, earned a decent living, and could fulfill the traditionally male roles in a relationship, such as taking care of car maintenance, repairing problems with the house, and managing yard work. As she looks retrospectively, she is not sure to what extent love played a part in identifying her first husband. In fact, she recalls what she heard older women say over the years – "a girl marries her father," and that seems to reflect her route to her first husband.

Although it was clear from the outset that Wysdom and her husband had vastly different approaches to life, she thought they were mature enough to keep them from becoming barriers in their united future. Wysdom was ready for children. Her biological instincts had initiated, with resounding force, the urge to procreate, in addition to which she just really looked forward to becoming a mother. She bore her first daughter in May of

1997 and her second in January of 2000. They became her focal point as it became clear that she and her husband were, in biblical terms, "unequally yoked" (2 Corinthians 6:14). Wysdom loved, and continues to love, church and her church community. Her husband was not a man of faith. Wysdom was social and wanted to immerse herself and their family in their community and social events, while her husband neither wanted nor enjoyed visitors in their house, outside of their immediate family. Wysdom wanted to travel to absorb the world and its beauty. Her husband was afraid to fly and allergic to something in each season of the year. Wysdom said, "Instead of living in marital bliss on a bed of roses, the marriage was like living on a bed of hot coals" where just about anything could trigger progressively more abusive behaviors. She decided she and the girls had to have a better life and left the marriage in 2005. She set up housekeeping in an apartment for a year, worked, and made sure the girls' education was not disrupted. Then, after ongoing appeals from her estranged husband and thinking it would be best for the girls to have their father with them, she acquiesced and returned to the marriage in 2006. Her intention was to try and make it work "for the girls' sake." However, she knew as soon as she returned that it was a bad decision. Every fiber in her being knew she had decided wrong, but it was too late. She had to stay since she had depleted her savings in leaving and setting up a separate household. She fulfilled the duties of each day focused on her children but felt as if she were buried alive. In trying to cope with the stress of the unhappy marriage and the demands of daily life, she turned inward to her faith.

Minister Michelle Chavers, one of the ministers at the Macedonia Baptist Church in Albany, New York, taught Wysdom the importance of prayer. Wysdom asked Minister Chavers to pray for her as she was going through the year of being back in a bad marriage. Minister Chavers stopped whatever she was doing and prayed right then and there. Right on the spot. Minister Chavers told Wysdom that when someone asks you to pray for them, you pray because you don't know what that person is going through at that moment and you don't want to miss it. Praying in the moment lets the person asking for prayer know they have been heard, and that their request has not been taken lightly. Minister Chavers also taught Wysdom the significance of praying aloud...not for glory but to articulate how you feel. Giving Wysdom license to speak her prayers was freeing for her because she was a verbal storyteller.

Wysdom's relationship with God, the Father, deepened over that tumultuous year to a point where she also wrote her prayers on paper. It became part of her daily ritual. First thing in the morning she would verbalize her gratitude and praise. As she went through her day, there would be times when she felt compelled by a spirit to write her prayers. It could happen anywhere and at any time. She could be at church or at her desk at work. When that spirit stopped by, she knew she had to take the time to talk with God...to have a conversation. She knew the Bible said to write down what I (the Lord God) will do for you...not as a to do list or a Christmas wish list. (*Therefore I say unto you, what things soever ye desire, when ye pray, believe that ye receive them, and ye shall have them.* Mark 11:24 KJV) She likes that she can go back anytime and read her written prayers. Reading them brought her a sense of peace when she returned to the marriage. She learned a format for prayers – she thanks God; gives Him glory; makes her request(s) known; reminds Him of what He told her in His word; puts scripture with it; and then celebrates the victory of her salvation in her relationship with Jesus in her prayer.

Sometimes she opens her journal and reads a prayer she wrote years earlier. The things she was requesting, the feelings all flow back to her. She can see where she has come from and knows that God brought her through the storms at that time and gave her whatever she needed. In retrospect, she can see how God answered her prayers. She does not have a designated "war room" or prayer closet, but when she needs or wants to pray, she prays. Prayer is such a part of her identity and her life that her family even knows when she is in prayer. She is emotional. She may be weeping or writing furiously. She just knows she needs to have a moment with her Father. In her prayers, she talks about things that she does not believe others would hear and understand. Opening a direct connection with God has been one reward of dealing with the struggles of a bad marriage.

Wysdom quietly suffered in her marriage through 2006 and into 2007, not allowing anyone, including her church family, to see the depth of her misery. However, being a woman of faith, Wysdom prayed without ceasing, as guided by 1 Thessalonians 5:17 (KJV). One day as she fought to maintain the facade she had established, she cried out, "Father this cannot be what you would have for my life!" That was a turning point for her. It became clear that she needed to leave the marriage. This time permanently.

Although people say, "Just leave!", in reality it was not that simple. You must know where you are going, how you are going to live, and where you are going to get the necessary resources to take care of yourself and your children. And then there is the timing. When do you actually walk out the door? Should it be when he is home or when he is out? Should it be during the week or on a weekend? During the day or at night? Her girls were young, and she had to protect them to the best of her ability. She began calculating what resources she would need to leave and provide a comfortable life for her children. Then Wysdom felt as if an invisible force began orchestrating her life. She likened it to the flow of driving in traffic when the light changes to green as you approach each intersection. Wysdom signed the lease and received the keys to her new home on Good Friday, April 6, 2007. She asked one girlfriend for assistance in moving. Over the course of that weekend, she and the girls moved out. By Sunday morning, the move was complete and Wysdom and her daughters were in church. Resurrection took on a whole new meaning for Wysdom on that Easter Sunday morning. Looking back, she is not sure how she and her girlfriend were able to move everything from boxes and furniture to a washer and dryer, but she knows the needed strength was a physical manifestation of her spiritual faith.

Wysdom had secured a new job in a different school district that paid more money, which allowed her to plan with some certainty, knowing she would have the necessary finances to support her family. Even though the new residence was located in a high-performing school district, Wysdom found the girls' assigned school's faculty, staff, and curriculum lacking in their ability to provide sufficient emotional or cultural support for an African American family. Wysdom was determined to find the right school for her daughters. In sharing her situation with her circle of friends, someone gave her the telephone number of the Albany Community Charter School. She made an appointment to speak to the school's parent coordinator and was excited to learn that the charter school's curriculum and culture reflected a focus on community. The school, with its before and after programming, parent and family involvement, and strong focus on academics, was exactly what she wanted for her daughters, so she immediately enrolled them. In addition, students at the charter school wore uniforms each day, which significantly reduced the stress about school clothes. Wysdom knew none of these developments were the result of her doing but came through her faith that God would provide what she needed.

It is 2018. The girls have matured beyond their years into accomplished young women. Wysdom tries not to dote on them too much but is extraordinarily proud of each of them. She has become an even more spiritual person and her prayer life is even richer. Over the years, her relationship with God has developed into an audible conversation and not just a written one. She can "hear" what He wants her to hear. She clarifies that it is not exactly like standard speech, but it is clear to her what His intent is when He speaks. What she likes most about this relationship is that she knows that if she can hear God, then God can hear her. This mutuality buoys her in times of trouble or uncertainty. She still prays aloud. At family prayer her older daughter recently exclaimed, "Mom, you're a prayer warrior! You can pray, Mom!" She took solace in her daughter's revelation, and one of her prayers is that each of her daughters is inspired to find their own prayer warrior within who will help them persevere through the challenges in life.

CHAPTER 7:

Without a Question

"For by grace are ye saved through faith;
and that not of yourselves: it is the gift of God."
(Ephesians 2:8)

Sharon F. will tell you her young life unfolded at her family's house, school, or church. She was an only child in the house but there was a sizable extended family of aunts, uncles, and cousins who seemed to regularly end up at her house. It was considered the gathering place whether she liked it or not, and whether she liked all her cousins or not! Since her mother and father were well known in the community and heavily involved in church, growing up, she felt the pressure of needing to "behave." That pressure, however, did not result in her necessarily being the ideal child. She recalls being mischievous more than meek.

Sharon F. remained an avid churchgoer as she grew into adulthood. Along with attending Sunday School and Sunday worship services, she played the piano and sang as far back as she can recall. She knew all the routines of church – order of Sunday service, hymns, Bible study, choir rehearsals – and followed them. The one thing that perplexed her was prayer. She prayed but she did not really understand prayer – how to pray or what exactly to pray for. She viewed God as analogous to Santa Claus in that you pray for something and God was supposed to deliver it. In young adulthood, she would pray for things and when they did not materialize, she would use that as evidence that God just was not real and return to doing things her way. She had her ups and downs living as she "faked the funk" at the time. In other words, she acted as if she knew what things meant such as Christianity, religion, and spirituality, but inside of herself was an uncomfortable void that she worked to hide from others.

For many people who adhere to a religious practice, it is almost impossible to pinpoint exactly when they knew they were on a faith journey. For Sharon F., that is not the case. She recalls the moment with clarity, although there is an element of spiritual mysticism in her revelation.

In 1987, while in her early thirties, Sharon F. worked as a security guard in Schaghticoke, New York, about twenty-two miles away from her home in Rensselaer, New York. As a single mother, she worked long hours to support three daughters. One night, after working a twenty-seven-hour shift, she was finally relieved by her replacement somewhere between 3:00 a.m. and 4:00 a.m. Exhausted beyond words, she still had to make the drive back to Rensselaer. She had made the drive numerous times and, if asked, would have said she could do it in her sleep.

She left the job and headed home. She recalls driving from Schaghticoke to East Greenbush, the town next to Rensselaer. As she neared home, she realized she needed to make a stop at the grocery store to buy breakfast food for her daughters. She thought if she brought milk and cereal, the girls would let her sleep a little longer. She had driven up Routes 9 and 20 to a cemetery that was a key landmark indicating she was close to home. That is when she believes she fell asleep behind the wheel of her vehicle.

The next thing she remembers is sitting on the couch in her living room! Where were her girls? The house was unusually quiet, and one question after another rolled to the front of her mind. Hadn't she stopped to buy cereal and milk for them with the hopes that they would get up, make it their breakfast, and let her get just a few more minutes of sleep? As she sat there, she slowly figured out that she had had an accident. But what had happened between the accident that left her with a broken nose, battered/bruised legs, a chunk out of her bottom lip, and missing a couple of teeth...and on the couch in her living room?

It came back to her that in what seemed like seconds after the impact she had regained consciousness with an, "Oh sh**!" At the time, though, she did not really comprehend what had happened. She just knew she needed to "Get out of this car." Somehow, she got out, but she does not recall how or the condition of the car. She noticed a house on the other side of the road. The business day for truckers was in full swing and they sped by in pursuit of coffee and something for breakfast at one of the many fast food restaurants on that section of the highway. She made it to the house and knocked on the door.

Based on the police report, her car had accelerated up a hill, veered into a telephone pole, hit a fire hydrant and ended up crashing into a garage that was built into the side of a hill. According to her parents, she was blessed to be alive since she was driving a sub-compact station wagon. They told her that because her uniform resembled that of a police officer, the couple in the house opened the door and called the 911 emergency number for an ambulance. The state police contacted her parents, and she was taken to the hospital. Those are the facts, but Sharon F. shared a different story.

Sharon F. remembers a "dream"...at least she calls it that. It was real to her. She was on or near Interstate 787, which runs parallel to the Hudson River, heading toward Troy, New York. The river was on her right. In her "dream," she was a small person, not in a car, and she so wanted to cross the river that sparkled like recently cleaned crystal. She was mesmerized by its beauty. The shore on the other side of the river seemed to be calling her name, inviting her to come behold its splendor. She wanted to get there.

Then a hand came down from the sky and grasped her hand. Although she could not see His face, inside she knew it was the hand of God. She tried to see His face, but He would not let her. Although His hand was strong, it felt gentle and comforting. Just the touch of His hand gave her a sense of safety, security, and love. She heard or felt Him saying, "I will never let go of your hand." That was the moment her spiritual journey began. She no longer had any doubt or questions about what she needed to do and felt a sense of immutable trust...faith.

She woke up a bit baffled on the couch. She had heard other people speak of "crossing over" in relation to someone dying. It made her wonder about wanting so badly to cross over the river in her "dream" and whether she had died or almost died. It felt so unbelievable, yet simultaneously unquestionable. She looked at her hand. It had been an automatic impulse to reach up to take that hand. Sharon F. recalls that when He took her hand and said He would never leave, it felt like a baby putting its head on the mother's shoulder...pure peace with nothing in the world to be concerned about.

Although the facts of the accident and its aftermath are undeniable, it was the "dream" that left Sharon F. undoubtedly knowing that what she sought in her earlier years was a real relationship with God, the Father. She realized that all the things she thought she was praying about, things she thought she wanted or needed in her life, all began with a focus on her and not on God, the Father. The accident was a transformative experience in that it propelled Sharon F. to search deeper and trust more. As a result of the "dream," it became clear to her that she had always had the power to change but had been using the wrong approach. The "dream" made her understand the importance of forgiveness. Before the accident, she thought just thinking something was "over and done and then moving on with life" was forgiving. She found, though, that that approach left her harboring ill feelings. Before she could move forward in deepening her relationship with God, she realized she had to start with forgiving herself. Her life had not been spotless. She had experienced what the world offered by way of pleasures...drinking, smoking, promiscuity. Now she uses herself as an example for others to know that regardless of how bad you think you have been, nothing interferes with building a relationship with God, the Father. Now, as she walks the path to becoming an ordained minister, her guiding question is, "What would God say to tell people to do?" She enjoys sharing the experiences that God has brought her through. She realizes that she can only direct Sharon F. and that God will take care of everyone else.

PART II:

HOW DEEP
IS YOUR FAITH?

CHAPTER 8:

How Deep is Your Faith?

"O give thanks unto the God of gods:
for his mercy endureth for ever."
(Psalms 136:2)

My growing faith sustained me as I continued on my life's path and was integral to my survival when life took me to another life-altering experience. In November 2002, two weeks after my 50th birthday, I survived a car accident that really should have taken my life. My car was totaled, and I ended up with a lot of metal parts in my body. More about that later, but what that experience taught me has taken years to surface. Psychotherapists and ministers, for different reasons, say when humans go through traumatic events, that our brains may neither absorb the significance of the experience nor possess the words to discuss it for many years, if ever. It has now been over eighteen years since the accident and now the words and thoughts come. It is as if a dam has been opened and I now have greater access to the bits and pieces and can begin to turn them into recognizable concepts and takeaways. At this point, I am still uncertain whether I have the full and accurate details that have been buried within my psyche. What I do know is that some things can be conveyed in words and, for other things, words are totally inadequate.

Physiologically, when your body sees a trauma approaching that you cannot avoid or conquer, the fight or flight reaction is activated. The part of the brain that "gives time and space context to an event [by] putting our memories into their proper perspective and place in our life's timeline" called the hippocampus, has been shown to become "suppressed during traumatic threat; its usual assistance in processing and storing an event is not available" (Rothschild, 2000).[21] Some psychologists and psychotherapists believe that this is the reason people often say they had a near-death experience. However, based on my upbringing and my religious beliefs, I must interpret my near-death experience differently.

The Times Union (Albany, NY)

November 2, 2002

COLLISION CAUSES RUSH-HOUR DELAYS

The article began, "Colonie: A crash between a car and an ambulance tied up rush-hour traffic near the airport Friday morning for several hours and left three people injured..."

People who hear about my accident often ask me questions. "Did you see it [the ambulance that hit my car]?" "Were you scared?" "Didn't it hurt?" "What did you feel?" "Were you conscious?"

People are intrigued by accidents, especially car accidents, in part because they are so very common. As we drive on our various highways and expressways each day, we see accidents. Ambulance lights, sirens, police vehicles, and tow trucks all mark the spot where an accident has occurred. As we drive past the scene, we crane our necks to try to see what happened and the extent of the damage. We quietly thank God it was not us. I was probably no different than you, until the day I was in the crash.

---

21 The Body Remembers: The Psychophysiology of Trauma and Trauma Treatment, Babette Rothschild, W. W. Norton & Company, New York-London, 2000, Pg. 12.

Even at that moment, I knew I had stopped traffic and somewhere someone was cursing at me for delaying his or her journey to work. I knew others were trying to see what the holdup was, how bad it was, and how long it was going to take to get traffic moving again.

As the Vice President for Applications of the Charter Schools Institute of the State University of New York (SUNY), at the time, I had been in New York City for several days facilitating a conference and then visiting and evaluating some of the charter schools authorized by the university. It was a job that was unfamiliar to most people – which was understandable given that such a position had not existed five years earlier. Charter schools had only been operating in New York State for about three years. The schools held students and teachers to a different, typically higher, standard when it came to teaching and student learning than most urban schools and some suburban ones. I, along with a couple of colleagues, had just completed a thorough evaluation visit using a multi-faceted rubric. While at the school, we focused intensely on indicators of effective teaching and learning. Typically, on visits, I did not get much sleep, as I would stay up late into the night reviewing information and data from the day. The days started early; we were in the schools no later than 7:30 a.m. and often did not leave until around 6:00 p.m. At the end of a two- or three-day visit, I raced for the plane, train, or car to head home. In New York City, it was off to Penn Station to catch the first train home. Sleeping on the train was a given.

The following morning was a beautiful Friday morning in upstate New York, November 2, 2002. I will never forget the date. The weather was splendid, with the thermometer reading in the high 40s. The sky reminded me of a pastoral painting with its calm but clear blue skies and bright sun with clouds appearing like whiffs of cotton floating silently above. For the northeastern part of the country, the weather was nice. I was always anxious to get to the office to respond to a mountain of emails and to begin downloading from my brain all the data and information gathered at the school. I could see the report forming in the back of my mind. Certain items were a no-brainer, such as basic school information – name, location, school leaders' names, student population, and performance data. But I knew analyzing the vast array of other qualitative information would take a while, along with ultimately developing objective and accurate statements regarding the school's operation and performance. I liked to get to it while everything was still fresh. I loved my work and the folks I worked with. I missed them when I did not get to see them regularly. They were like a family...my work family. I double-checked that I had what I needed to head to the office, positioned my tea mug in its holder in the car, and secured my briefcase carefully in the back seat. I slid into the driver's seat, locked the doors, and fastened my seatbelt. As usual, I checked to make sure everything was in order before I backed out of the garage and closed its door at my regular time around 8:15 a.m.

The street was clear and orderly. It is a nice, quiet neighborhood with lots of trees. Our backyard borders on a forever-wild area so we often had an array of nature's residents visiting...deer, foxes, wild turkeys, rabbits, squirrels, opossum, and occasionally a skunk or two. My husband, Scott, and I had searched hard to find such a place within close range of shopping, the airport, the expressways, and especially our friends. We loved our house and neighborhood. I felt blessed each day when I think about how fortunate we had been. How many people could honestly say that between their network of friends (church and work) and the beauty of nature they felt embraced by the world they inhabited?

As I pulled out that morning onto the main route to the expressway, the roads were dry and clear. I merged into traffic and quickly got up to speed. I took one of my two typical routes to work that both ended up passing the airport. All was moving along well with no backups or accidents. The drive to my preferred entrance to the expressway was pleasant with its smooth curves. I liked the feel of the car as it glided along the road. I had driven this way to downtown Albany hundreds of times over the years. Sometimes I wondered why the car did not just automatically find its own way. Traffic was moving along at a good clip without any impediments and I felt so alive.

The curves wound past the airport. It looked as if the morning commuters to places like New York City, Boston, Washington D.C., Pittsburgh, and Syracuse had jammed their cars into every available space in the airport parking lot. I was glad I was not heading off on any of the popular morning commuter flights, and that I was making steady progress in my fifteen- to twenty-minute commute downtown.

Just as I thought things were moving along nicely, I approached a traffic signal slightly past the airport entrance. I could see the light change to red. I began to slow down, anticipating that I would need to stop. I was in the right-hand lane. There were cars, and other vehicles, behind me and beside me in the left lane. I still am not sure whether I had come to a complete stop, or whether I had just slowed down to the point where a slight touch of the brake would do it. I was first in the line of cars at the traffic signal. The light changed from red to green. I looked to my left to check traffic but could not see anything because a large vehicle was directly beside me. I did not see or hear anything unusual, so I began to pull out.

Just as I pulled forward, I glanced left again as my window cleared the front of the vehicle to my left. I was shocked to see a full-size ambulance bearing down on me. It was surreal. My mind could not fully comprehend that the situation was not a scene in a movie. My mind swirled through probably every defensive driving technique I ever knew trying to connect them to what actions my hands and feet needed to take. Turn the steering wheel away from the ambulance? Speed up to avoid being hit? Stomp on the brake and pray the ambulance misses me? There was no time to do anything. The next thing I recall was hearing the loudest explosion I can ever remember hearing. It resounded within my head. BOOM!

Suddenly, it was dark. I do not know if the car spun or turned over. I do not know where the car was in the intersection, and I did not care. I was someplace that was quiet and peaceful, almost sweet. I felt nothing. I think I died. Time seemed non-existent, and I had no sense of my body...meaning I was not aware of my limbs and whether they were responding to my commands to move. I was neither cold nor hot but comfortable and at peace. I felt that I was floating and could be anywhere in the universe. It was a place I wanted to stay. Although I felt whole, I did not feel confined to a physical body. I began to easily move through the air without any limitations. The colors around me were hues that defied description – golds, creams, purples, mauve. As I felt the lightness of me, I also felt a sense of welcome and acceptance. I did not see anyone or anything, but I became aware of a question being posed to me. Not verbally but clear, nonetheless. I understood it. I was asked whether I wanted to stay. I had a choice.

I thought about my daughter. She was about to turn eighteen years of age and had just started college in September. She still needed me. Abruptly, the peace was disrupted. I either said or thought, "Breathe!" "Breathe!" "Breathe!" I gasped for air and sputtered to get dust out of my nose and mouth. "Breathe!" "Breathe!" I blinked my eyes to clear my vision. I felt as if I was being born again. Taking my first breath. The more I told myself to breathe, the clearer my vision became. As the fog lifted from my mind, I realized what had happened to me.

It seemed that each second was extended and lasted several minutes. This different realm of time allowed me to recall everything happening with some level of detail and specificity. Perhaps this increased time was not a good thing because it let me clearly see the shattered glass, to smell the metal being cut, and to feel the cold of the November day. What was probably seconds seemed like an eternity.

"Were you scared?" No. Fear did not enter my mind. I watched. I assessed my condition and responded to questions being asked by the emergency workers. I remembered what I had learned in meditation – how to be still. How to go deep within and be peaceful; how to focus on the breath. That became my silent mantra: "Breathe." "Slowly. Deeply." "Inhale." "Exhale."

"Oh, my God!" This cannot be real, but it was. I felt calm. Everything around me moved at a frenetic pace. I sat still just concentrating on breathing. Something wet and warm ran down my face. From all the glass I saw around me, I figured it must be blood. For a second, I tried to see the damage to me physically. I began to take inventory of my condition...right hand and arm...I can move them! Good! I feel the toes on my right foot, but my legs are stuck together between the dashboard and the console. I feel the toes on my right foot, but nothing else. I cannot see my right knee. Oh well. I can feel the toes on my left foot and can slightly move my left knee. Good! Somewhere inside I knew I would be fine, so I relaxed. Perhaps it was shock, or I was delirious.

A woman was talking to me. Where was she? She was standing outside the back passenger-side door. I do not know what she said. I talked to her, telling her that she really needed to call my husband, and that my cell phone was in my purse. I told her the telephone number. I guess she dialed. I remembered that my husband was headed to a friend's home to help put up a shed. The woman said she got the answering machine. I then asked her to call my office. I did not know whether she did or not because an emergency technician had gotten into the passenger seat in the front. He began asking me questions. "Do you know your name?" "Do you remember what day it is?" "Do you know what happened?" I answered all his questions and then turned my attention to what was physically going on with my body. My left

(Courtesy Albany Times Union, November 2, 2002)

arm hurt, and the pain increased exponentially if I tried to move it. The emergency technician instructed me to stay still. Even so, I wiggled in my seat just to see if I could feel anything else. My tailbone moved, and it did not hurt. I was encouraged.

The nerdy part of me wanted to look around and see everything. I wished I could step outside my body just to see what the car looked like and what exactly was going on. Someone put an oxygen mask on me, and it was difficult to breathe because blood from my head kept getting under the edges of the mask. Then someone would empty it. Whenever I tried to turn my head, the emergency technician would tell me to be still. The technician was a nice, reassuring man. He watched me intensely. He cut the sleeve of my jacket and sweater to insert an IV (intravenous injection of solution) into my right arm. He took my vital stats – heart rate and blood pressure. Somehow, I had managed to move my head either before the emergency technician entered the car or at some point when he looked away from me. Although it felt as if I could easily develop a headache, my neck felt fine. After doing my own self-assessment to the best of my ability, I turned my full attention to following the emergency technician's directions.

I heard much commotion outside my car. I could not really see, though, or perhaps I did not really look. I saw my shattered windshield. It looked as if my steering wheel was hanging by a thread. My dashboard was so close to me I could touch it without needing to straighten my arm. One of the men working to extricate me from the car got in the seat behind me; he told me even though there was going to be a lot of noise, I would be safe. He told me they were going to cut the door and roof off the car to get me out; he said to let him know if anything hurt. Another person put a protective cover over me to prevent any more glass from injuring me. The crew outside sawed the metal and pushed and pulled to get the dashboard away from me. Then suddenly the dashboard shifted, causing pressure and instant and intense pain. I screamed, and the guy behind me hollered to let them know to stop whatever they were doing. All kinds of directions and questions were being bandied about outside the car as the workmen figured out how to remove parts on my car. In addition to moving the dashboard, they were trying to determine how to remove the headrest. I could not make out the discussion of various approaches and which one was ultimately used to take the headrest off. Once the headrest was gone, they put a collar around my neck. It was not long afterwards that the front of the car seemed to relax and released me.

The emergency technicians' discussions then turned to how best to remove me from the car. I was informed of each step of the process. I began to feel the cold as I was put on the stretcher and wheeled to the waiting ambulance. All I saw was a beautiful blue sky. The whole thing was so reminiscent of a movie. I saw the ambulance doors as they raised the gurney and slid me in. Inside looked just as I recalled an ambulance I had seen on television – spotlessly clean, neatly secured equipment, and medical paraphernalia. Even before I was secured in, the ambulance technicians began their work: double checking my vital signs, telling me who they were and where we were headed. One technician sat still and began to question me: "How are you feeling?" "What, if anything, hurts?" "What do you think is wrong?" He told me that he would be in communication with the hospital as we traveled. I told him I thought my left arm was broken. He said he was not sure, so he cut the sleeve of my jacket and sweater on that arm. I wanted to tell him to stop since it was my favorite jacket. His face showed me that I had been correct in my diagnosis. I did not know how badly the arm was broken. I knew that even at the slightest touch my pain increased dramatically. He asked his partner which stabilizer would work best on my arm. They came to agreement quickly, and promptly apologized for causing additional pain as they placed my arm in what appeared to be a large Styrofoam hot dog bun.

I continued my mantra, "Breathe...breathe..." The bleeding from wherever had stopped, and I did not need the oxygen mask emptied again. The emergency technician often reassured me that everything was going as intended, and that I was in good hands. The two of them talked about my right knee and leg, but I could not hear well enough to understand what was being said. They talked with the hospital a couple of times during the ride to the emergency room. I do not recall what they did to my knee. I could not feel anything from the knee to the foot.

Once the emergency medical technicians and I arrived at the hospital, I was rushed from the ambulance into the emergency area. All I could see, since I could not turn my head, was the ceiling. In my peripheral vision I noticed people moving past the gurney as it moved down a hallway. When we stopped moving, we were in a large area with several medical staff. People did a variety of things, some of which I am sure I was completely unaware. I was poked and prodded all over my body. My chest was X-rayed to see if my lungs were punctured or ribs broken. Fortunately, the lungs were fine, but my ribs were bruised. Glass pieces were all over me and smashed into my clothes. Every time I was moved, more pieces were found. I continued to find pieces for several days.

Scott, my husband, had arrived at the hospital while I was being evaluated and we waited for the results. My daughter, Simone, unexpectedly popped around the curtain. I had not wanted her to know of my accident until I had been cleaned up, for fear it would be too much for her. But there she was. I was happy to see her, and I could tell by her face that how she reacted was deeply dependent on what I said. As she got closer, I smiled as best I could. She called out to me, "Mom!" "Mom!" She leaned over close to my face, and I reached for her with my uninjured arm. I told her that I would be alright, and that seemed to calm her fear immediately. She then got busy checking me out and everything around us, especially my right knee.

What does remain fixed in my memory is the assessment of the damage to my right knee after the other tests had been completed. The doctor or intern asked if I could bend my right knee. Although I did not feel the muscles working in my right knee, I somehow managed to bend my knee. He and other staff cleaned the area by flooding it with a sterile solution. My husband informed me much later that it was "a lot" of solution. With my right knee bent, the doctor asked me if I could lift my right foot. I said I would try. I tried, and tried, and tried. He had me try, at least, three times. All unsuccessful. My daughter later told me that each time I tried more blood would gush from the open wound.

Multiple X-rays were taken of my left arm and right leg. That was the most painful part of the evaluation of the damage to my body. One lone female X-ray technician was on duty at the time. She had to both position me and take the X-ray. She told me I would be there a while because she had to take a lot of X-rays. It felt as if I was there forever, and it was cold. She did eventually finish her job and wheeled me back to the emergency room, where my husband was waiting. I was relieved to see him. He was both concerned about my physical condition and relieved that I was alive.

Scott, Simone, and I waited again for a period of time as X-ray results were read, and consultations were held about my condition and medical needs. Finally, the findings were shared with us. The good news was that my lungs were not punctured; however, both bones in my left forearm were badly broken; my right kneecap was shattered into six or seven pieces; and the tendon in my lower right leg was severed. There was a contusion on my forehead about the size of a plum that would take some time, but it would go away. The bruising of my ribs and tenderness of my left side would eventually heal. Time would also heal the various cuts and scrapes on my body. The bones had to be repaired, and the doctor was preparing to do three surgeries immediately.

As all of this was occurring, members of my faith community and other friends had begun gathering in the hospital's waiting area. My husband and daughter provided periodic updates to those waiting, including my pastor. I remained in the emergency room for an unknown amount of time before being whisked off for preparation for surgery. The preparation steps are not clear in my mind. I met more medical personnel, such as the anesthesiologist, nurses, and residents. Last, before succumbing to the anesthesia, my orthopedic surgeon introduced himself.

It seemed as if I took a short nap, but in reality I had been unconscious for hours. The nurse was talking to me, asking me if I was thirsty. I was parched! She provided me with cold water by dipping a small sponge on a stick into a glass of ice water. Who knew how incredibly refreshing that would be! This was recovery. As I became less groggy, like any curious individual, I wanted to "feel" my arm and leg to see what kind of condition they were in. My left arm was in a plaster cast from just above the elbow down to the knuckles of my left hand. I could move my shoulder. My right leg was in some sort of removable, metal-reinforced nylon cast. I had never seen anything like it, and I could not fully see this one since sitting up was out of the question.

My husband was finally allowed to see me in the post-op area. The orthopedic surgeon spoke to us. He told us that he had had to do some bone grafting to help the bone grow across the large gap between the ends of the broken bones in the left forearm. Each bone in the forearm now had a metal plate with six screws each holding it in place. He also told us that he had put a screw in the right kneecap to hold the two major pieces of bone together and used metal wire to rejoin as many of the smaller fragments as possible. He had to discard some of the pieces because they were too small to be of any use. The tendon was essentially sewn back together. Overall, he said all went well. The removable cast on my right leg was there so they could keep a close check on the leg for any infection since it had been an open wound. He said he would see me the next day.

It was probably 10:00 or 11:00 p.m. by the time I was assigned to a hospital room. I had been prescribed morphine for pain management to use through a self-medicating drip dispenser, and I pushed the button for a droplet or two every half-hour or so when I was awake. I slept for hours. However, hospital noise starts early, about 5:00 a.m. each day. How anyone gets a full night of sleep in a hospital is beyond my comprehension. Whenever I awoke, I was extremely stiff, sore, hungry, thirsty, uncomfortable, and to top it off I had to go to the bathroom. Oh God. How do I do that? A bed pan, of course. Trying to lift my lower half to get on the bedpan, using my good arm and good leg, without losing my balance, was a challenge of Olympic proportions. It got easier over the next couple of days. Thank heaven.

The pain medication dispenser and I became good friends, and I felt no pain. I tired somewhat quickly and napped off and on throughout the day. Many friends came to visit during my six-day hospital stay. At times, I had as many as six people in my room. I napped, though, regardless of whether I had company. They loved me enough to tolerate my sleeping.

Monday morning, day four, physical therapy began! I had to learn how to use my uninjured extremities to move from bed to chair, from wheelchair to chair, or probably most important was wheelchair to potty! Right leg and left arm were out of commission, so no walking or doing anything that even hinted at a possibility of falling. I would be unable to catch myself without inflicting further injury. The surgeon told me that had it been a simple break in my arm, he would say two months before I could begin using it again. However, because of the severity, I was probably looking at three months. For the right knee, he prescribed no weight bearing, at all, for at least, six to eight weeks. At the end of that time, he would make a determination. That news, although expected, really placed limitations on how I would move forward over the next few months.

I learned quickly to balance on my good leg to navigate between my bed and the portable commode, and between my bed and the moveable chair. I was extremely careful not to lose my balance and fall. The wheelchair navigation skills I had learned early in my life at twelve and thirteen came back to me, just like riding a bicycle again. The only difference was that this time, I could not use both hands.

The body is an utterly amazing instrument. Hospital staff installed a traction system over my bed to hang a "triangle" for me to grab to assist in lifting myself. The good arm quickly began to strengthen as I used the device multiple times per day. My desire to become as independent as possible as soon as possible was a welcome incentive by the physical and occupational therapists at the hospital. Once again, just as at twelve and thirteen, everything presented another "challenge."

On day four, my pain medication dispenser was taken away, which made me wonder how much I really needed it. I had developed a sense of security having easy access to pain medication. That day I found that I was just incredibly tired. Hospital staff, family, and friends reiterated that I had been through a traumatic event. Funny, as much as I knew intellectually it was traumatic, I did not feel as traumatized as those around me felt or expressed. In fact, I felt quite light and happy. Must have been the morphine.

Bright and early the next morning, day five, the orthopedic surgeon's resident came in and removed the cast on my left arm. I was astonished. The excitement was short lived. The removal was just to allow the doctor to look at his work. I too took my first look. When I first saw my arm, it took my breath away. I thought of Frankenstein's stitches and scars. It was bruised and scraped, with scabs everywhere. Steri-strips were aligned up and down two sides of the forearm, covering the stitches making it look like a small airplane runway. The doctor was pleased with its appearance. The incisions were straight and neat. I told the doctor that he had been quite tidy. He laughed. Then just about as quickly as the cast had been removed, a new cast replaced it. The doctor was not concerned about infection in the arm since the broken bones had not broken through the skin; it was a closed break.

At some point on day five, I heard the first mention of "going home." The possibility surprised and frightened me. Although I wanted to be home, I was not physically ready to be home. The physical therapist wanted to work with me another day to ensure that I could satisfactorily use the equipment. In addition, I needed certain equipment at home, such as a hospital bed, wheelchair, portable commode, and a hemi-walker for support. The doctor approved the equipment for home, and that set the wheels in motion for ordering the various items.

Throughout each day in the hospital, friends came to visit. As each one came, I found that there was a certain cathartic process that had to occur. People needed to tell me how this event had affected them and what actions they had taken in response to the news. Major accidents are more than just collisions of vehicles and resultant injuries to the occupants' physical bodies. Major accidents, often life-threatening, involve immediate families, extended families, friends, close and not-so-close acquaintances, neighbors, those who treat the injured – doctors, technicians, therapists, nurses, co-workers, unknown friends of co-workers, church and organizational friends and acquaintances, clergy and lay leaders, and total strangers. In fact, as I have grown through this experience, I discovered that my accident did not just happen to me, but it happened to everyone who touched my life.

I thought, at first, that it was only because the accident was fairly recent in everyone's mind that when they saw me, they had to talk about it. They talked about where they were when they heard "the news"; how they felt; what they did; who they told; who they saw who knew me; and what they told that person. They talked with disbelief, but thankfulness, that I had survived.

As the days turned into months of recuperation at home with multiple outings each week for physical therapy, I began to physically heal. Each time a guest visited me at home and after five months when I began to re-enter some of my routines, every time I bumped into someone who had not seen me since the accident, that individual had to go through their experience with me. It became clear to me that that was part of the experience for us all. I began to facilitate the sharing of their experience. It was important that each one have a chance to go through it with me and for me to hear their words.

Someone told me that when they heard about the crash, they could not believe it and they wondered, "Why Jennifer?" The person said, "I know I should not, but I wondered why you? You are a good person." Bad things do happen to "good" people and, in my case, I was finding that that was a question on many people's minds. Why would I be exempt from anything? The question seemed to puzzle others much more than it bothered me.

That is what love can do. It connects each of us. What happens to one member of a family or group happens to each member. It could not have been more clearly demonstrated through my family and friends. I would find months later that individuals who had not seen me in the hospital still needed to connect with me on that level, even though I had moved on.

By the end of day five, I had truly mastered a multitude of self-care activities. I could transfer from the bed to a wheelchair (and vice versa) or portable commode without assistance. I could get on and off the bedpan that I used at night. I could wash myself except for my back (which would not happen for several months to come). I could feed myself using my uninjured right arm. I was feeling pretty good about life, the world, and everything in it.

Morning rounds on day six brought the surgeon in for a look at me. He liked what he saw as my body had begun to heal. He wanted to keep checking on the right knee. There was a good possibility that it would become infected, but the left forearm was in the plaster cast to stay. I was told that my wheelchair and hemi-walker (a hybrid between a cane and walker that is lightweight and used at the side instead of in front of one's body) would arrive later in the morning. Also, I found out that the hospital bed and portable commode would be delivered to my home that very day as well. Once the physical therapist showed me how to safely transfer to and from the wheelchair, and I had my second "shot in the belly" (as I called the anticoagulants), I could go home. Unfortunately, the second shot could not be given until after I had eaten dinner! So as anxious as I was to leave, it was not going to happen early in the day.

In reality, I probably should have stayed another day, but, as most patients, I just really wanted to go home, and the insurance was not going to cover the cost of an additional day. I went after dinner. Therein started a long recuperation process, with Scott giving me shots in the belly at home for a significant part of the following week.

Since the day of the accident, people thought I was rather upbeat for being in such bad physical condition. I smiled, talked, and laughed while in the hospital. I am not sure what visitors thought...maybe my good mood was the result of the pain medication. I felt peaceful but looked a wreck. I had a plaster cast on my left arm, and a removable cast on my right leg. I had a knot on my head, bruised ribs, and two black eyes. How could I possibly feel good? But I did.

In fact, I felt guilty for feeling so good. I remember telling my husband that whenever I talked to people about the accident, I actually felt quite happy. A lightness came over me that was extremely peaceful, and I just felt happy as if the joy of life itself filled me. It was difficult for others to understand and believe when they visited me at our home. Friends would often enter the house looking at me with sympathy as if I would break. Then I would tell them about how I felt, and slowly their spirits would lift, and they let go of their preconceived notion of how I should look and feel. It is interesting to watch others watch you.

Miracles happen every day to many people. It was miraculous that I had lived and that I was not in severe pain all the time after I stopped taking medication. Don't those qualify as miracles? My physical body certainly was a mess. I felt no pain, and after two weeks I took no more pain medication. My body healed faster than doctors anticipated and ultimately after a year I had no visible traces of ever having been injured. There has been much research on the relationship between healing and faith. Brian E. Udermann in the *Journal of Athletic Training* talks about The Effect of Spirituality on Health and Healing: A Critical Review for Athletic Trainers. Dr. Udermann found the "research on healing and recovery closely parallels the research reported for general health...evidence shows that the stronger one's spiritual commitment is, the more likely fast and effective healing and recovery will occur."[22] And spirituality can be viewed as one function of faith.[23]

Some people would say I am lucky. I personally do not believe in luck. I believe in a gracious God and have faith that He will bring me through life's struggles. I learned many things as the result of this accident. It would take me pages to list all my takeaways, but

---

22 *The Effective of Spirituality on Health and Healing: A Critical Review for Athletic Trainers*, Brian E. Udermann, PhD, ATC, Mesa State College, Grand Junction, CO in the *Journal of Athletic Training*, Volume 35, Number 2, June 2000, pp. 194-197.

23 *Faith, Spirituality and Religion: A Model for Understanding the Differences*, Leanne Lewis Newman in The College of Student Affairs Journal of Baylor University, Spring 2004, Volume 23, Number 2, Special Edition on Faith, Spirituality and Religion on Campus, pp. 102-110.

I will share some of the major ones with you. Now I know that:

- God and angels are with you always and they never lie.
- You often appreciate others more when you are almost taken away from them.
- Others often appreciate you more when you are almost taken away from them.
- My husband, Scott, is truly an angel on earth.
- Every second is a gift and could be taken away at any moment.
- It is difficult, if not impossible, to carry a cup of hot tea or anything else when you walk using a walker.
- Other people can be extremely generous with their time and their love.
- Not being able to walk can interfere with everything if you let it.
- A flight of stairs can seem the size of a mountain.
- You can do just about everything with one hand to care for yourself, except in my case my hair, opening containers, and cutting food/meat/anything.
- Patience is indeed a virtue.
- It is sometimes difficult for other people to accept where you are and the condition you are in, even if you do.
- Most people want to be helpful.
- Wheelchairs are wonderful inventions.
- Portable commodes can come in really handy.
- The words I use can contribute to someone else having a good day.
- My family and friends truly love me.
- Being independently mobile is a real present.
- The mail person and delivery guys are typically nice people.
- I can order just about anything on the internet for delivery to my door.

▸ The most important parts of life happen on the inside, not the outside.

▸ Peace is an inside phenomenon.

The choir at my church sings a song called, "I Need You to Survive" by Hezekiah Walker. The words resonated so strongly with me when I heard it during my recuperation that the song brought me to tears, especially where it says, "I pray for you. You pray for me. I love you. I need you to survive." When you are incapable of praying for yourself, I believe it is the prayers of others that sustain you. Prayers which are an expression of faith come from love, and love is what connects us. At the second my car was hit by the ambulance, I was incapable of doing anything on my own. God and the angels took the reins and made me breathe again. Word of the accident spread at lightning speed through a grapevine of friends that I did not know really existed until that time. The web of friends created a cushion of prayer on which I could rest and physically heal. It was the prayers that gave me energy and strength. Prayers from others – not me. I needed them to survive.

Research has found a strong correlation between prayer and healing. In his book, "Why Faith Matters", David J. Wolpe refers to the work of Dr. Harold Koenig of Duke University who summarized his findings regarding the benefits of devout religious practice, particularly involvement in a faith community and religious commitment, by saying that "people cope better...they experience greater well-being because they have more hope, they're more optimistic... They have stronger immune systems, lower blood-pressure, probably better cardiovascular functioning, and probably a healthier hormonal environment physiologically... And they live longer..."[24] In addition, Mr. Wolpe recognized that "faith-

---

24 <u>Why Faith Matters</u> by David J. Wolpe, 2008 (Published by Harper One), p. 182.

based healing is not part of an organized religious program...but demonstrates yet again the force of allowing transcendence – or God by another name – into one's life."[25]

If you were asked the question, "What can your faith withstand?", how would you answer? It is often said we can withstand and heal from more than we know. The following stories take you through circumstances that test that premise. The situations made individuals question their faith – if they claimed having faith at that time.

---

25 Wolpe, p. 183.

CHAPTER 9:

Peace be Still

"And he arose, and rebuked the wind, and said unto the sea, peace be still. And the wind ceased, and there was a great calm."
(Mark 4:39 KJV)

People carry "stuff" with them – high school embarrassments, secrets from relationships, family hurts – and sometimes traumatic events from which they have physically recovered, but the event is forever etched in their memory.

Young Terry had an idyllic childhood, raised in a Christian home with both parents who she thought were the "smartest people in the world." They taught her from an early age that she had every right – like anyone else – to live her life, learn all she could, and be whoever she chose to be. Her father was very clear that she should let nothing dissuade her from getting a good education. In addition, she recalls the freedom and freshness of living "in the country" in Gloucester County, New Jersey. Her family lived next to a farm, where they gathered fresh fruits and vegetables for meals almost every day. She remembers being able to run and play in acres and acres of fields and open land, and the state having vast areas with nothing but farms. And she never needed an alarm clock since the neighbor's rooster dutifully woke them each morning. This is the life she misses at times.

In elementary school, Terry was smitten with a love for the theater. She attended Gibbstown Elementary School, a primarily White school (1st through 8th grades) in the 1960s, so racism and prejudice were a common part of life for African Americans. At assemblies, White children did not want to sit next to her, so she sat next to the teacher. The one thing at school that was pivotal in her life was each Friday one of the classes was responsible for producing a play for the whole school. In the 3rd grade, her class chose to produce *Little Red Riding Hood*. She wanted to try out to be Little Red Riding Hood. She knew in her heart that she would make an excellent one. She also knew that she had as much right to fill the lead role of Little Red Riding Hood as any other student in her class. However, such was not to be. Her teacher told her she could not play that role but that she could play the wolf. She took this disappointment and made the best of it. She decided to be the very best wolf the school had ever seen.

The week following each performance, student representatives from the remaining grades would come tell the performing class how much they enjoyed and appreciated the previous Friday's production. When representatives came to share their reactions to her class's rendition of *Little Red Riding Hood,* each representative commented on how great the wolf was. This experience was her introduction to theater and sealed her lifelong involvement in the theater arts.

Terry continued through the public schools of Gibbstown, New Jersey. During her high school years, she recalls that her mother had a recurring dream. In her mother's dream, someone was trying to hurt Terry, and her mother had to grab that person by the shoulders to physically stop him from holding her daughter down. Terry's mother had this dream repeatedly to the point where Terry felt bad that she could not help her mother end the dream cycle. Her mother continually prayed about the dream, and towards the end of Terry's junior year in high school the dream stopped. Terry believes God let her mother know that everything would be taken care of and that is when her mother no longer had the dream. Terry graduated from high school in 1975.

She moved to New Brunswick, New Jersey, where she attended Douglass College, an all-female college within the Rutgers University system, and where she would ultimately have both faith- and life-defining experiences. Terry graduated from college in 1979 and found a job in Edison, New Jersey, but lived in an apartment in East Orange, about a fifty-minute commute. However, her stay in Edison and East Orange was short-lived. Her mother was diagnosed with terminal cancer and Terry returned home to be with her and her father. Her mother died ten months after her college graduation. As she worked through the grief of her mother passing, she contemplated what to do and where to live. New York City and its ever-vibrant theatres, shows, and productions called to her and she responded. She took a job at the J. Walter Thompson Advertising Company by day, but fully indulged her theater passion by studying with the Negro Ensemble Company and the Frederick Douglass Creative Arts Center during every other waking moment.

While living in New York City, Terry and a female friend from college days attended the Canaan Baptist Church on 7th Avenue in Harlem. That friend pestered her relentlessly each Sunday to attend a college reunion at her alma mater, Rider University in Lawrence, New Jersey. After a month of pleading, Terry's resolve gave way. She reluctantly succumbed to her friend's request. Her friend arranged a ride for them with another friend to the reunion. That friend was male. His name was Greg. That ride was the beginning of a life-long relationship between Terry and Greg.

About a year and a half into working for J. Walter Thompson Advertising, Terry's father was in a car accident and suffered significant injuries. Having lost her mother, Terry was beside herself with concern for her father's well-being and felt compelled to move home to care for him. Once he recovered, she returned to New Brunswick, New Jersey, taking a full-time job at the Crossroads Theater Company. New Brunswick was where she lived when she was invited to join Greg and his family for Thanksgiving dinner in 1989. She asked his family what she could bring to contribute to dinner. Although she does not recall what item his mother requested, Terry recalls being so excited that she forgot to pick it up. So, on Thanksgiving Eve, around 11:00 p.m., she quickly put on her white coat hanging nearest the door and jumped in her car to make a run to the twenty-four-hour grocery store. She had done this plenty of times and thought nothing of it.

It was a beautiful night with snow lightly falling, perhaps a couple of inches on the ground. The world seemed very serene as the snow twinkled in the moonlight. She ran into the store, purchased her items, and was back in her car in no time heading back to the apartment she shared with two roommates. As she sat at a stop light, she noticed that the streets were completely empty. She thought no one else was crazy enough to be out at that time of night on the evening before Thanksgiving – November 22, 1989. Suddenly, the stillness was broken when her passenger side door opened, and a man hopped into her car. The man smelled of liquor. She noticed that he had a bottle wrapped in a brown paper bag in his hand.

Terry's heart started pounding and her mind raced to think of everything she had ever heard or seen about what to do if accosted by a stranger. Even in the midst of thoughts swirling in her head, she realized that none of the scenarios she recalled included being behind the steering wheel of a car. She immediately started bombarding the man with questions – "What are you doing?" "Why are you in my car?" "What do you want?" The man cursed at her and told her to just drive. She was terrified beyond words and drove on in an autopilot mode. She was in shock and the stillness amplified the sound of the man's voice. However, she knew she could not afford to panic. The man ranted and raved in his drunken state, so he did not notice when she unfastened her seatbelt. At the next traffic light, she quickly opened her door, jumped out of the car, and ran. The man, even in his condition, moved with such speed and agility that he was out of the car in an instant even as the car continued to slowly roll forward. He forcibly snatched her, threw her into the front passenger seat of the car, and jumped into the driver's seat. He was now in control. She wondered why he had not just taken off with the car. He would have had her car and her pocketbook. She had to figure out what to do and fast, or she knew this situation would not end well.

Her attempt to run away had infuriated the man and, in what sounded almost like a growl, he told her if she tried anything else, he would kill her. She peered out the car window and noticed the man was slowly heading toward some dumpsters in an isolated parking lot. She quietly said, "Lord help me!" Her hand went down between the seat and the door and fell upon the neck of the bottle he had brought into the car. When he parked the car, she yanked the bottle out of the paper bag and smashed it across his face as hard as she could. She did not wait to see his reaction. She leapt out of the car from the passenger side and started running. Terry was in such a state of shock that she did not notice her shoes had come off and she was running barefoot. With each step, she could feel the frozen ground on the soles of her feet, but she did not care. At this point, she only knew she had to run as fast as she could and scream as loud as she could. She thought she had a good head start, but again, as if he had tentacles, the man grabbed her and fiercely tackled her to the ground. Snowflakes flooded her nostrils as her face was pressed to the ground. Even with her now blood-stained white coat on, the cold penetrated her whole body as she struggled to free herself. The man's size and weight negated any possibility that she could escape. The man, now seething with anger, leaned close to her ear as he sat on her back. Terry could feel his warm blood dripping on her head and seeping through her hair onto her scalp. He told her her escape attempt was "cute," but now he was going to kill her. He wrapped his arm around her neck, and she thought, *This is it. I am going to die.*

Thoughts flooded Terry's mind and it raced to process them all, but chief among them was the thought that her father would not know where to look for her. She pleadingly cried, "Jesus!" In that instant, when she called Jesus' name, it was as if someone had taken the man by the collar and lifted him up and off her. She felt relief from the pressure of the man's weight as she twisted around in the snow expecting to see that someone had happened to come by at that moment and pulled the man away from her. Even in her panicked state, she thought it was good that she would now have a witness to the vicious act. As she thrashed about to a sitting position, she looked but was confused by what she saw. No one else was there. The man was not just on his knees but was actually standing straight up with blood running down his face from the bottle cuts. He stood there as if frozen in time and space.

Young Terry did not hesitate. She ran. She ran screaming and barefoot into a wooded area, sustaining cuts and bruises along the way. She ran until she saw lights. Houses. She did not look back, but the man had not chased her. She ran to a house and banged on the door, pleading for help. A man opened the door. As it turned out, the man was a police officer. As if she had to empty the contents of her reeling mind, the details of what she had just experienced poured from her lips. She could see the man's wife and two small children in the background. The children were holding on to their mother's leg as this woman from the dark, cold night barged into their house. Terry says she must have looked "a sight." She wonders how this family let her in not knowing whether she might be dangerous. The man called the police station while the wife found some socks for her feet and blankets to wrap around her.

The police came and put her in their car. They drove back to the location where the man had first tackled her in the parking lot, but the snow had covered any traces of the attack. All that could be seen was blood on her coat and back of her hair from when the man had pinned her to the ground with his arm around her neck. They took her to the police station to file a report.

SUPPLEMENTARY INVESTIGATION REPORT

1A. Department Perth Amboy	2A. Mun. Code 12/6		4A. UCR	21. Prosecutor's Case No.		22. Dept. Case No.		☐ Co-op ☐ Original
5. Crime/Incident Theft of Motor Vehicle		3A. New Crime/Incident if changed		23A. Victim's Name/New Address if changed				
5A. New NJS		7A. Date of Crime		Terry L. Green				
			ADDITIONAL VALUE STOLEN PROPERTY	40A. Currency	41A. Jewelry	42A. Furs		
			43A. Clothing		44A. Auto		45A. Miscellaneous	
46A. Additional Stolen Property Value	7A. Additional Recovered Property Value	1/23/89 47A. Teletype Alarm		49A. Add'l Technical Services		50A. Technician and Agency		
51A. Weather rain	52A.	53A.	54A.		55A. Evidence ☐ None		56A. Disposition	
57A. Chem. Lab. No.	58A. Ballistics Lab. No.	59A. Survel Wstn No.	60A.	Yes No ☐ ☐ Blotter ☐ ☐ Retained ☐ ☐ Obtained ☐ ☐ Surveyed		Yes No ☐ ☐ Arrest Pending ☐ ☐ Teletype Pending ☐ ☐ Evidence Pending		

List chronologically of Previous Arrested/Summoned — Complete Information on How Arrested/Summoted — Include Additional Perpetrators — Suspects — Record of Developments Since Last Report — Explain any Crime Change — List Additional Interviews of Victims — Person Contacted — Witnesses — Evidence — Technical Services — Stolen Property — Recovered Property — Court Action — Prisoner Dispositions — Attach Additional Statements — Victim Property Loss Report, Etc.

11. No. Arrested −O−	31A. New Arr'st	62A. Adult	63A. Juvenile	64A. Curr. Status Crime	155. Curr. Status Case	66A. UCR Status	11A. Date Cleared
16A. Name		ADDRESS OF ARRESTED/SUMMONED			33A. Age	39A. Sex	71A. Race	73A. D.O.B.

No suspects

12/6/89, 8:48 AM Detailed to Smith st. & Gifford st., recovered stolen vehicle, upon arrival spoke to above Terry L. Green of 150 Elizabeth ave., Paulsboro N.J. who stated while driving in Perth Amboy at above date & time she located her 1988 Chevrolet, 2 door, color white, NJ reg. EOC-265, VIN# 1G1GZ1120JP106439 which was parked in front of 323 Gifford st., this officer spoke to resident at 323 Gifford st. a Mary Cervony who stated above vehicle had been parked in front of her residence for approx. 2 to 3 weeks.

Victim stated she was driving her vehicle through New Brunswick at 12:30 AM 1/23/89 when a

A. Rank/Name (Print or Type) Matthew Mercurio Signature	71A. Badge No. 180	75A. Page 1 of 2 pages	77A. Date of Report 12/6/89	77A. Reviewed By
	76A.	79A.	80A.	81A.

CONTINUATION PAGE

	2. Mun. Code	34. Prosecutor's Number		22. Da.
Perth Amboy	1216			

black male approached her vehicle and entered same through the passenger door and told victim not to get out of her vehicle.

Victim drove to Edison where she grabbed a beer bottle the suspect was holding and struck same with the bottle. Victim was able to flee her vehicle and reported incident to Edison Police and the New Brunswick Police.

When vehicle was located by victim and this officer the keys were still in same as well as blood samples and broken bottle fragments.

Above indicated ___ the Perth Amboy Police Garage and preserved for further investigation by Perth Amboy Det. Kudrick and Dets. from New Brunswick Police.

13. Print or type Matthew Mercurio	34. Badge Number 180	75. Page 2 of 2	76. Date of Report 12/6/89	77. Reviewed By
Signature	78.	79.	80.	81.

It was 12:30 a.m. on Thanksgiving Day when she completed filing the police report. She did not think of calling anyone – not her roommates, her parents, or her boyfriend. She just wanted to get home, so the police agreed to take her to her apartment. As she rode in the police car, she remembered that her keys and her pocketbook with her identification and address were in her car... which the man still had.

Terry arrived at her apartment disheveled, cold, and shaken. She woke her two roommates from deep sleep as they grumbled that it was the middle of the night and wondered why she was waking them. Once the roommates cleared the sleep from their eyes and saw the condition Terry was in, she had their full attention. Terry told them everything that had happened. The roommates tried to comfort her as best they could and offered to remain up for the duration of the night. She sent them back to bed, but she stayed up the rest of the night, worried that the man would come to her apartment. He did not. Later that day she and her roommates found a locksmith who would work on the holiday and had the locks changed. Terry went to dinner with Greg and his family as if nothing had happened – not disclosing any of the events of the previous evening.

Terry did not want to tell her father. She could not even figure out how to start a conversation about the attack with him. Initially, Terry told her father that the car had been stolen. Because of their closeness, her father was aware that she had not told him the truth. He did not pressure her for more information. She believes that he understood that when she was ready, she would tell him the truth. Her father rented a car for Terry to use to travel to and from work. The weight of not telling her father the truth was heavy on her mind, so near the time to return the rented car she decided to go home and tell her father what had happened. It was one of the most difficult things she had ever done. Her father's head was bowed as Terry, weeping, shared the details of that night with him. When she finished her story, her father, who was a Christian man, sat there stupefied. He said very pointedly, "I would not have spared his life." As grueling as it was for both Terry and her father, it was a great relief to Terry to tell her father the truth.

A few days after the attack, she called the police station to see whether the man had been found...whether they had found her car abandoned someplace. Neither the man nor her car had been found. She called frequently thereafter to check since no one was calling her. Over time, the policeman answering the phone started responding to her questions as if she were an annoyance... as if she had done something wrong. She understood why women who were raped were reluctant to go to the police.

Then she decided to gather information on her own to help the police solve the case. She started calling local hospitals under the guise of being a detective investigating the abduction of a young woman on a certain night and the alleged perpetrator had been injured. She asked whether the hospital had any records of an admission that night of a Black man with facial lacerations. She called numerous hospitals with no results until finally the last hospital she dialed said they had a Black man come in with facial lacerations. They gave her his address.

She drove to the area where the man lived, thinking she might see her car. She drove and drove, circling several blocks numerous times. Nothing. When she was about to give up, she turned a corner and there sat her car. She went to get the police.

When the police arrived, one of the neighbor ladies came out of her house saying she had no idea where the car came from. She said it had been parked there for two or three weeks. She admitted that she thought the car had been stolen and that she should have called the police herself. The police towed the car to the station and examined it. They found broken glass and blood on the steering wheel, indicating that the man had been injured. Terry's pocketbook was still in the front seat. Nothing had been taken from it...nothing missing...keys and wallet undisturbed. The officers on duty took a report asking who found the car. The other officer responded that Terry had found the car. The police took fingerprints from the car and gave it back to her.

Terry updated her father about the car. They cleaned it up and she continued to drive it. The police had Terry look at pictures of possible suspects, but she did not recognize any of them. Sometimes the police would try to coerce her to identify someone from a picture, but she never did. The police never found the man, so for quite some time Terry feared that he might appear one day. He never did.

Terry, now Deacon Terry, can still vividly see the man standing over her as she scrambled to her feet. As she thinks about the attack and her escape, she remembers the dream that her mother had for all those years. Her mother prayed and prayed about the dream and its outcome. Deacon Terry believes her mother had the dream until she knew her daughter would live through the attack. Deacon Terry knows that it was the Lord who held the man in that moment and kept him from harming her. She says it "felt like" the Lord's presence. Deacon Terry says, "When I called the Lord's name, He showed up!" She believes without a doubt that the Lord saved her, just as He performed miracles in biblical times, such as saving Shadrach, Meshach, and Abednego from the fiery furnace (Daniel 3:23-27). She also believes that her survival demonstrates that God honors prayers – prayers from our mothers, grandmothers, aunts, whoever – as well as from us regardless of the amount of time between the prayer and its application. Other than the police reports that were filed at the time, you will not find a paper trail to prove or disprove Deacon Terry's beliefs. She has lived many years beyond the traumatic event and over those years has come to have a much deeper faith and understanding of the power of the spirit. Deacon Terry is convinced that "if the Lord protected me then, I know He will protect me now."

CHAPTER 10:
In His Way

"And the peace of God, which passeth all understanding,
shall keep your hearts and minds through Jesus Christ."
(Philippians 4:7 KJV)

People sometimes say that big gifts often come in small packages. In this case, that gift is Sharon. When we met to talk about her transformative faith experience, it struck me how petite she really is as I stood to hug her upon her arrival. To see Sharon, one cannot help but notice how precise she is in her dress and mannerisms. She sat gracefully and tilted her head ever so slightly when speaking. Each hair on her head seemed to know its place and stayed there. Sharon listened intently when I spoke and responded without hesitation to the questions. As a writer, how do I relay a story of something so intimate and devastating to a parent, a family?

Sharon began. "My daughter, Shonye´, was a normal kid growing up." But as we talked, she shared that her daughter had been born almost two months premature with one collapsed lung and the other had a cyst. The doctor at St. Peter's Hospital in Albany, New York, said there was not anything they could do for her baby. She and her husband were overcome with despair. Their hearts were heavy as they sat after hearing the prognosis. It seemed out of nowhere a woman came into the room. She looked like a staff person – a physician, nurse, or some other medical personnel. They were not sure, but when the woman said, "We can save your baby if you take her to Albany Medical Center," they did not need to hear another word. This was especially true since the doctor at St. Peter's had told them that their daughter was getting worse. They wasted no time in transferring Shonye´ to Albany Medical Center. To this day, neither Sharon nor her husband have been able to locate that woman. They have looked through records and any documents that might provide any insights to the identity of the woman, but to no avail. The woman appeared when they were in need, met that need, and vanished. They prefer to think that she was an angel sent by God to fulfill a mission and when that mission was complete, she moved on to her next assignment.

Sharon and her husband are glad they took Shonye´ to Albany Medical Center because the staff there did indeed save her. Not to say that Shonye´ did not undergo a variety of procedures and tests, but Sharon and her husband were, and are, so thankful for the outcome. They were at a point where they thought they would lose their daughter before she even had a chance to experience life.

In fact, Shonye´ lived life in a manner that many people aspire to. She was not afraid to try new or different things – running track, playing baseball, traveling. In her 11th grade school year, 2000-2001, Shonye´ traveled with her school class to Spain and Africa. She was creative and figured out how to do the things she wanted to do, letting nothing get in her way. However, in the latter part of Shonye´s senior year in high school something was amiss. She began to complain of back pain. Her parents took her to the doctor. Back therapy was prescribed. Shonye' continued going to school and even attended her Senior prom, although silently bearing intense pain. After prom, in addition to the pain in her back, the pain intensified and extended into her arm. On Mother's Day, her parents took her to the emergency room. They learned that Shonye´ had a rare form of lung cancer that had metastasized to other parts of her body, which is why she experienced pain in her back and arm. The doctor told Shonye´ and her family that she would need to start chemotherapy and radiation treatments immediately. She did undergo chemotherapy and radiation treatments, but the disease moved aggressively. Shonye´ was eighteen years old in 2002 when she transitioned from her earthly body.

Initially after Shonye' passed, Sharon was just mad. Mad at everyone who appeared to have failed her daughter – the doctors, the hospital – and God. Hadn't she and her family been praying? Sharon recalls being in a fog in the early years after Shonye´ passed. At times, she could not remember normal, everyday things and events such as going grocery shopping, picking up dry-cleaning, making appointments, or returning phone calls. She said she does not recall what she did other than go to work and come home.

Five years passed before she could sit and think about her daughter, her life, and the impact of going through the death and grieving process. She learned a lot about grief. She learned that if one does not allow themselves to go through it, it will interrupt you when you least expect it. As she worked through her grief, she realized that she had prayed for God to remove Shonye´s pain, and He had in His way. Now she understands that with the peace of passing, Shonye´ is no longer in pain. Sharon came to the understanding that she had been blessed to have Shonye´ for eighteen years...years that from the conditions of her birth, with one collapsed lung and one with a cyst on it, were almost taken before she first left the hospital.

Sharon's faith has led her to believe that God needed Shonye´ and that Shonye´s life continues to help other young people. One critical observation from Shonye´ as she went through cancer treatment was that there was not anyone of color on her care team of doctors. In 2003, Sharon and her family established a scholarship for students of color interested in pursuing studies in the medical field. It is a private scholarship that allows students to use the funds however necessary to support continuing their education.

Sharon now sees life in a different way. She has faith that whatever happens is part of God's plan even if the life circumstances or events do not align with one's personal plans. She also operates each day with unconditional love for people as the foundation for everything she says and does. Sharon grew up going to church. She was in the choir, learning to play the piano and assisted her mother in directing the choir. She attended Sunday School, worship services, and special programs – the whole package. In retrospect, she realizes she was not a bad person but was just going through the motions of living the Christian life. She had not made the connections between what the Bible said and how she lived life. Now she knows that God is real; she feels Him. She cannot explain it in words but, having gone through the living and transitioning of her daughter, Sharon has a totally transformed feeling for life and people. Ultimately, Sharon says, "Everyone has to have their own experience to actually 'get it'" and make the connection between words and behaviors."

CHAPTER 11:

Rooted

"Blessed is the man that trusteth in the Lord,
and whose hope the Lord is."
(Jeremiah 17:7 KJV)

Life has a way of making or breaking people if they do not have deep roots. Roots are what hold trees up and keep them from blowing over in high winds and storms. Sometimes the roots are not deep enough and when the storm is raging, the tree falls. Karen's roots are deep. She has weathered, and is weathering, life's storms. She is strong in her faith that God loves her. When asked to share an experience that significantly impacted her faith journey – something that let her know that there is something bigger than herself, something that transcends what we see, what we think we know and what exists beyond our knowing – Karen had multiple stories to tell.

Karen started with her childhood and what she has come to know and understand as an adult. As a young child, she did not understand why her father left the family. She was three years old when her parents split up. She and her mother moved from Philadelphia to New York City in 1973. Her mother thought her father was having an affair, but he was instead chasing a love of the high from heroin. When Karen was in college many years later, she learned that her father hid his addiction well enough to function during the day. He worked each day but would get high in the evenings. As she reflected on the view through her childhood eyes, it all made sense. When she would come to visit him, the two of them would do fun things in the daytime like go to the park, play games, or go on trips, but he would always nod off in the evenings. She thought he was just tired. She thought about the many times he had promised to visit her over the years but never showed up...times when she would wait up for him until her mother made her go to bed. Her mother knew he was not coming, although he had the best intentions. His "love" held him back.

The main story Karen wanted to share related to an accident she was in in 1993 when her car was pushed across four lanes of traffic. At the time she was practicing Islam, although she had been raised as a Christian. She was on her way to pay her car insurance premium. If she did not pay it that day, the policy would lapse at midnight. She had begged and pleaded to get the money from her then-boyfriend. He gave it to her at the last minute. This was the boyfriend her friends and family wanted to see her without, especially since he was already married. She admits it was a crazy situation, but he was so persuasive. He had convinced his then-wife, who was not Muslim, to not only accept that their relationship included Karen but to actually prefer that the relationship include the three of them. Ultimately, he promised Karen that he would divorce his current wife and marry her as his second wife. Looking back, it is hard for Karen to believe she fell for such a set-up.

Karen lived in a rural part of New Jersey at the time, and the route to the insurance company's office included a two-lane highway where driving 55 miles per hour was legal. She arrived at a corner where she had to make a left turn onto a four-lane road. Another car headed in the opposite direction had stopped and indicated that he too intended to make a left turn. As she proceeded to turn, a third car came speeding around the stopped vehicle, not seeing her car in the intersection until it was too late. The speeding car slammed into her car. The impact was so strong that it pushed her car not only across the two lanes heading the intended direction but also across the other two lanes heading in the opposite direction! Across four lanes of traffic! As she watched the lanes of traffic flying past her eyes, as if on a merry-go-round, she cried out to God – not Allah. She knew in that moment that she had to return to her roots, to Christianity.

Ambulances were called to the scene of the accident and Karen was removed from her car onto a stretcher. When the ambulance arrived at the hospital, the emergency medical technician said she was delirious because she had been speaking gibberish during the ride. She argued that she was not delirious but praying in a language they were not familiar with, and that she was aware of everything that had happened to her and around her. Karen and her boyfriend had learned Arabic through classes they were required to take as part of a political/religious organization named the Nuwaubian Nation. The organization operated under different names over the years, such as the "Ansaaru Allah Community (AAC)" (Council of Public Liberal Arts Colleges (COPLAC) Digital 2018) and the "Children of Abraham" (Dwight York n.d.). The organization taught followers a faith based on the ever-evolving worldview of its leader, Dr. Dwight "Malachi" York. The teachings incorporated pseudo-Islamic, pseudo-Judaic, Black nationalism, extraterrestrialism, and other theories of the day, but maintained a consistent focus on Black separatism. All members had to learn Arabic in keeping with the AAC's pseudo-Islamic beliefs, and especially to pray in Arabic. Karen, as well as many other young people in her area, had been drawn to the social relevancy presented by the Nuwaubian Nation (Council of Public Liberal Arts Colleges (COPLAC) Digital 2018) and were unaware of the various criminal allegations against the organization.

That moment of clarity as her car spun across traffic set Karen in motion to re-claim the God she knew and to leave the boyfriend. During the year following the accident, Karen questioned the teachings shared in the required classes; the classes no longer made sense to her. She knew there weren't two gods and that she did not need to pray to two. All that she had taken in about the Nuwaubian beliefs was stripped of its authenticity. It took another year, but she ended the relationship with her boyfriend and her relationship with the Nuwaubian organization.

Another transformative faith experience involved an accident that took Karen's son's life. Her oldest son, Daniel, was a sergeant in the military and had just graduated from nursing school as a Licensed Practical Nurse. He had completed a tour in Iraq and returned home to his wife and two daughters, age one year and age five months at the time.

It was Sunday, April 15, 2012. Karen's phone rang. It was her daughter-in-law, who she had finished talking to moments ago.

Her daughter-in-law was screaming and crying. Karen heard, "He's gone! Daniel is dead!" Karen dropped the phone and fell to her knees, praying to God to bring her baby back. She prayed to have God raise him as He did Lazarus in the book of John (John 12:1-17) if it be His will. Her brain scattered, trying to process what she was hearing over the phone.

It was the weekend, and Daniel had been out with four friends riding their motorcycles. Nothing unusual. They rode with two riders in front, two in back, and one in the middle. On this trip, Daniel was in the middle. Karen and her family have yet to understand how Daniel crashed head-on with an SUV with that configuration. To this day, no one is exactly sure what happened and how Daniel was the only one who suffered and died. One and half years after the fatal accident, it was discovered that no autopsy had been performed. Daniel was stationed at Fort Belvoir, but he and his family lived off-base. The military assumed that the civilian authorities would handle the situation while the civilian authorities assumed the military would take care of everything that needed to be done relative to investigating the accident. As it turned out, neither organization followed through and there was no investigation. Karen continues to seek God's peace in putting the lack of details to rest, but she is without a doubt that Daniel's death was anything but an accident. She believes there is a purpose and plan for each of us through God's word.

Karen's faith has deep roots. Her mother and grandmother were both Bible-reading and Bible-quoting women. As much as Karen tired of them telling her what "the Lord said" whenever she strayed, the lessons were lodged deep within her. Her grandmother instilled in her that the day one is born and the day each of us is to die is written. Karen's understanding of that reference is that our birth and death are pre-ordained in the Book of Life, which Karen interprets as holy or divine. Karen knows God has seen her through the various storms in her life – not growing up with her father, her car accident in 1993, the loss of her son Daniel, a subsequent car accident in 2018 and the loss of another son, Savion, in 2018. She says there are ongoing issues in her life that she knows God helps her deal with and situations in which she is thankful for the support she receives from her family at Macedonia Baptist Church. Karen rests assured that "God's got me."

CHAPTER 12:
Stronger Now

"And the Lord said, if ye had faith as a grain of mustard seed,
ye might say unto this sycamine tree, be thou plucked up by the root,
and be thou planted in the sea; and it should obey you."
(Luke 17:6 KJV)

Ollie often wonders why. Why her sister was killed in a car accident when she was only nineteen years old. Why her father left the family when she was in 3rd grade. Why it seems so difficult for families to "get along." She came from a large family with nine children including her three brothers and five sisters. She was the "knee baby," meaning next to the youngest. Because there was such an age difference between her and her older siblings, her nieces and nephews are about her age. She was more of a sister than an aunt. Ollie remembers playing with her nieces and nephews. She recalls a lot of love in the house as they grew up.

As brothers and sisters matured and went their separate ways, in her early thirties Ollie's path led her to a relationship with a man who came to Albany, New York, and she came along – almost for lack of anything better to do. At the time, they had been together for about ten years, but the relationship was not a good one. Nevertheless, she stayed and found a job as a nurse's aide. She really liked being a nurse's aide and helping people. She worked as one until a freak accident in 1998 forced her to stop.

She was transferring a small female patient from a chair to her bed, which was higher than it probably should have been. The woman was teeter-tottering and Ollie wanted to make sure the woman did not fall and hit her head on the bed's headboard. She was determined to move the woman in a way to avoid that happening. Ollie did, but in the process, she hurt her back. She reported the incident to her supervisors and kept working. She worked for several days until one morning her alarm rang; she tried to get up but could not. Excruciating pain shot through her body when she tried to stand up. Her fiancé came to help her, and she ended up at the doctor's office. Based on an X-ray, the doctor's diagnosis was a sprained back. The doctor wrote the note for Ollie to be on medical leave from work for six weeks. She returned to work the seventh week but found she was still in pain whenever she attempted to do anything that involved physically managing a patient.

Her nurse manager sent her back to the doctor, who this time used MRI (magnetic resonance imaging) to see Ollie's spine in detail. The results showed that she had a bulging disk that needed to be surgically removed. What she did not know at the time of the surgery was that the doctor did not replace the bone with any type of support. This meant there was nothing between the vertebrae. Over time, the disks wore down and began pinching her nerves again. She needed more surgery to alleviate the pain. In 2010, Ollie underwent spinal fusion surgery, during which synthetic bone material was placed between her vertebrae with the goal being that the vertebrae would grow together as one unit. The procedure temporarily alleviated the pain, but not on a long-term basis. Ollie was prescribed physical therapy and participated for an extended period of time. She now walks with a cane and has less pain, but she is not totally pain-free. Regardless, she is thankful to be upright.

Even though Ollie has been through experiences that might have resulted in her being bitter at this point in her life, she is thankful for many things. One of the many things she considers as a blessing is coming to Macedonia Baptist Church. Near the end of 2002, her neighbor told her she just had to visit this church with him. She did and has been coming ever since. She joined the church and was baptized on January 4, 2004. She calls it the "greatest day of my life!" The people of Macedonia, in Ollie's words, are "loving and kind...even though they don't know you. If you are in trouble, they'll be there for you." She views Macedonia members as her "family" who were, and are, there when she needs them and have always been good to her.

An experience she did not understand until she was more grounded in her faith occurred when her fiancé was shot. She did not know he had been shot, as she does not usually watch television news. It was Saturday night, July 16, 2005. She had spoken to him that evening, and then she went about preparing for church the following morning. She received a call around 3:00 a.m. on Sunday from his phone. She kept saying "hello," but she only heard people talking in the background...asking questions like, "Did you see this man shot?" She hung up and went back to sleep, assuming he had accidentally dialed her number. When she arrived at church the following morning, one of the deacons was waiting on the steps for her. She knew something was wrong but figured she would check into it following service.

During the sermon, something kept telling her to look out the window. The church had beautiful large windows with some including stained glass. Ollie is very sure she saw her fiancé ascend into the sky. She recalls seeing his face as if he were there to tell her himself that he had transitioned. She recalls being in awe of seeing a white angel in the bright sunlight. Ollie could only make sense of these images as the day unfolded.

Following service, she and her nephew planned to drive to New York City to return her niece's car. As they got into the car, Ollie's phone rang. It was her fiancé's brother asking whether she knew he had passed. Until that point, she had not. The news spread quickly that Ollie had lost her fiancé, and Macedonia members, Ollie's family, stepped in to support her.

Before coming to Macedonia, Ollie admits she was not angelic and that she had done things she should not have. One of them was smoking crack cocaine. She was addicted, but even then the Bible was her guide. She lived the paradox of knowing what was right but being physically addicted to something that was wrong. She says she was "playing with both the devil and God." When she became overwhelmed with the addiction, she turned to the 23rd Psalm, "The Lord is my shepherd; I shall not want...Surely goodness and mercy shall follow me all the days of my life; and I will dwell in the house of the Lord forever [King James Version]." Reading the verses was comforting...peaceful...and helped her stay away from other people using drugs at least for a short time. Even while she was in the world of drugs, Ollie still believed in God.

One day while living in Albany, a friend gave her a package of crack cocaine to sell. She asked him why he would trust her with a package that she might smoke. She was perplexed. He said he trusted her. Little good that did because she smoked half the package. She sold what was left. She told her friend and apologized for what she had done. She told him that she would give him the cash from what she sold and that she would give him anything except things from her house like her television, VCR, or music. Ollie knew then that she had to quit.

Just as Matthew 25:13 and Mark 13:32 refer to man not knowing the day nor the hour when the Son of God will return, Ollie does not remember the exact date or hour that she ultimately made the decision to quit drugs. She knows it was a Sunday in the summer and, in retrospect, that it was God who stepped in to give her the power she would need to make it through what was about to happen. She headed for her room, locked the door, and stayed there. She went through withdrawal in that room. Ollie says she thought she was going to lose her mind in that room. She heard things and became paranoid at one point but did not come out. She only came out to go to the bathroom. She cannot quite recall all the details but knows she probably did not eat for a couple of days. She slept a lot but would wake and read the Bible. She cried and had many conversations with herself to remain focused on getting clean. She told herself that she had to "shake it off." Even in the throes of breaking from the grasp of addiction, Ollie knew there was a God. She says she knew "there was something greater than me!" Even though she was physically alone in the room, she knew God was with her the entire time.

As the days passed, she began to come out of her room. Over two or three weeks, she cleaned her house and made a plan to get a job. She told everyone who typically hung around her house that they had to go elsewhere because she was not having any of the drug activity in her home. She has not smoked crack since her withdrawal experience in her room. No rehabilitation. No twelve-step program. Now she understands that if "your faith is strong enough and you really want it, it can happen because God is real and will give you the strength to endure the most difficult situations."

CHAPTER 13:
Overcome Evil with Good

"Be not overcome of evil, but overcome evil with good."
(Romans 12:21 KJV)

Slim was born in the Brownsville section of Brooklyn, where people such as Al Capone and Murder Inc. lived and "worked." Brownsville is where he learned the difference between a gangster and a thug. A gangster was considered a businessman who didn't want problems in the neighborhood or the police nosing around, while a thug tended to be a young guy somewhere between the ages of sixteen and twenty-five who carried, and often used, a gun to resolve any issues. Even with the likes of such well-known figures living in his neighborhood, Slim loved Brownsville. There was a strong sense of camaraderie, a neighborhood structure with many community development organizations and strong Baptist churches. He had a good life in Brownsville, even though there were nine children in his family and space was at a premium in a two-bedroom apartment. He grew up with both of his parents, who were ministers, and they both had jobs. In fact, his father worked multiple jobs with his primary job being in "uniformed services" (one of the many city government service departments, i.e., water, sanitation, police, etc.). That job paid the most and provided health insurance for his family. His mother worked in the garment district as a presser and often came home with burns on her arms from the large pressing machines. Sometimes she worked as a seamstress, but that was not her favorite. His house was a stable home where an emphasis was placed on education, family values, and religion. However, the expectation was that by eighteen or nineteen years of age at the latest you were out of the house and on your own. There just was not any room. As he thinks about it, though, two of his brothers managed to remain at home into their twenties. Slim is not sure how his brothers convinced his father to allow them to remain at home, but he recalls that his father was very clear that they definitely could not stay at his house without having jobs.

With education being such a focus for his parents, it was crucial that Slim be able to read and read well. In elementary school, he was promoted from one grade to the next until 5th grade. In 5th grade, he was held back by an African American male teacher, Mr. Thompson, who explained that his reading was not up to par. He was not reading and understanding as well as he should have been at that point in his development. Slim was, of course, devastated but Mr. Thompson, who he liked and respected, promised to work with him to improve his reading. Slim recalls one positive aspect of having to concentrate on his reading was that he had more time to be with his father. His father, who was in his mid-forties at the time, had not mastered the skill of reading. So, as Slim grappled with and conquered the fundamentals of reading, he taught his dad. He remembers sitting at the kitchen table and his father asking him about his reader. This memory often brings tears to his eyes...this was special time that he had alone with his father. With nine children in the house, having any private time with his dad was almost unheard of. They would sit at the table, just the two of them, with his father questioning him about the various nuances of reading and Slim helping his dad eventually become a proficient reader. He treasured these moments.

When Slim started 5th grade for the second time, Mr. Thompson was again his teacher and he aggressively worked with Slim to improve his reading and comprehension. That year, 5th grade was a totally different experience for him and the skills that he gained allowed Slim to excel as he moved through the school year. In fact, he did so well academically that when he entered junior high school in 8th grade he was placed in the advanced Reading/ English class. Another teacher, Mrs. Thompson (unrelated to Mr. Thompson), ensured that he was on the college preparatory track during junior high and senior high school and facilitated him graduating early.

Slim's life, in his opinion, is replete with experiences where he is sure it was God who intervened on his behalf. Slim had an experience when he was about fifteen years old, probably in 9th or 10th grade. He had come home from school and was relaxing and processing the events of the day. As he teetered between being awake and asleep, he heard a voice speak to him. He recalls not hearing it with his ears but in his mind. At first, Slim thought he was being called to the ministry because the message told him to help people, especially young people. Although he believed in God, Slim resisted the possibility that he was being called to ministry since at the time he enjoyed occasionally participating in smoking reefer and having a taste of wine. He thought if the message had been a call to the ministry, his taste for worldly pleasures would have ceased or, at least, significantly diminished.

A few years later, when he was around nineteen years old, through the New York City Police Athletic League (PAL) he did coach a baseball team of teenagers (thirteen- to fifteen-year-olds) to a city baseball championship. The team beat the champions of the four other boroughs to bring the win home to Brooklyn. Slim attributes that experience and the opportunity to work with those teenagers as something resulting from God's intervention in his life.

As Slim neared high school graduation, he submitted applications to several colleges and was accepted at three. However, the family's funds were limited so he went locally to Brooklyn College....at least to start his post-secondary education. In the fall of his freshman year at Brooklyn College in 1973, Slim went to visit a friend who attended Middlebury College in Vermont. The campus, with its classic granite and limestone buildings located between New York's Adirondack Mountains and Vermont's Green Mountains, was so majestic that it could have easily been featured on the cover of an art magazine. While at Middlebury, Slim was fortunate – no, now he says he was blessed – to meet the dean. He was deeply inspired by this African-American man who served as the dean of a predominantly White Ivy League institution of higher learning. The dean told him to bring his transcript on his next visit. Slim agreed to do so and returned home. When he next visited his friend after the winter term, he took his transcript. He does not recall all the details between bringing his transcript and applying for admission. What he does remember is that he was accepted into Middlebury College. He could not believe it. In addition, since the tuition was so high, he qualified for financial aid. His parents were so proud. He is not sure how they did it, but they managed to contribute some money toward his attendance. For Slim, being admitted to a small Ivy League college, getting financial aid, and his parents contributing to his attendance was a totally unexpected turn of events in his life.

Slim tried out for the football team at Middlebury College. He was fast and could run a 40-yard dash in under 4.4 seconds...maybe 4.5 seconds. However, the dean was not about to let football have the best of him. The dean was all about academic performance, and so was Slim's father. Slim came home one semester with two Ds and two Bs. The school's policy allowed a student to only have five Ds on his or her record during the full four-year college experience. Slim earned grades that were split with a B for content but an F for spelling and grammatical errors. On his visit home with the two Ds and two Bs, his mother reassured him that everything would work out. His father, however, took him to the basement and said, "Negro, if your grades don't come up next year, you're going to the army! You are my ninth child, and I am tired! I'm done! Don't tell your mother we had this conversation." He did focus after that "conversation" which, he says with a smile, was basically a monologue by his dad. He made sure he was taking the right courses. He did play football, and he brought his grades up to As and Bs. Ultimately, he graduated on time from Middlebury College...a far cry from Brooklyn College.

The Brownsville side of Slim has always influenced what he does and does not do. Smoking reefer and drinking wine went with the neighborhood, and as a young man he wanted to be part of that life. However, not only was he a minister's son and his family very involved in their community, but he and his friends were athletes. They had to be careful not to do anything that might negatively affect their performance or involvement in sports. They remained on the fringe of the drugs and drinking activities in the neighborhood, occasionally having a drink or smoke but never allowing themselves to be considered regular participants. Some of their friends, though, were deeply involved in more illicit activities. Whenever Slim and his athletic friends were out in the neighborhood with those who were regularly involved with drugs and drinking, they were very adept at knowing when to part company to avoid being connected with any illegal activities.

However, a couple of years after graduating from college, Slim started dating an older woman and she seduced him more deeply into the drug culture and the "sweetness" of cocaine through freebasing. When on a cocaine high, every sensation was amplified and made him want to stay in that realm forever. That relationship ended after a few years, but over the next ten years, Slim's success in staying away from the substance ebbed and flowed. He would stay clean for a while and then it seemed that it was always a "friend" that would re-introduce him to cocaine, insisting that it was "in his best interest." During his drug years, he thought he was functioning "normally," but the reality when he looks back is that the addiction affected all parts of his and his family's life.

Slim had a college degree, landed a state job with the New York State Division for Youth, and earned a good salary. He married, bought a three-story brownstone, and had three children. Life was good. As a family, they visited various churches in Albany's Capital Region often based on meeting and talking with various ministers who worked for the Division. They attended an African Methodist Episcopal (AME) church for a while. Slim could relate to the minister. The AME church, however, seemed a bit too structured.

Reverend Comithier was one of the ministers that worked for the Division. Slim had met and talked with him a few times when he had come into the central office but did not know him well. Nevertheless, he decided the family would visit Macedonia Baptist Church in Albany, New York. They found the church atmosphere and the members welcoming and felt comfortable. They started attending more regularly.

Slim had not been attending Macedonia very long when his three-year-old son came down with chicken pox. His family had a history of having severe reactions to the disease, and his son was no exception. He had a fever of 102-103 degrees over a two-day period. Slim and his wife used alcohol baths to try to cool his body down, but to no avail. They ended up taking him to the hospital and taking turns staying there with him. Slim looked up at one point and saw this man walk in the room. It was Reverend Comithier, pastor of Macedonia. Reverend Comithier sat down with Slim and his wife and started praying. They held hands as they sat there in his son's room. Comithier prayed and then prayed some more, probably for ten to fifteen minutes. Rev. Comithier prayed so strongly that his entire body shook. The strength of the pastor's praying reminded Slim of times he had witnessed his mother praying when he was younger. Although the pastor's visit was totally unexpected, Slim and his wife were very thankful he had come by. The next day, his son's fever broke. Slim told his wife that they were going to become part of Macedonia because the pastor clearly was good with the Lord. Without a doubt, he said, "The Lord knows who Comithier is." Slim has never left Macedonia in over thirty years and has no intention of going to church anyplace else.

In 2015, Slim had another experience that left him questioning whether the message was real or an illusion. Either way, the message was clear to him that he needed to work on the one project that had eluded him for years – helping children. In this instance, he was in his bed asleep, but he saw what he perceived as the hand of God. It looked like it was surrounded by a bright light and it was illuminated in a way he could not explain. Then he saw that the hand was attached to God's arm. His arm came down and lifted him and other people up. Although Slim could not see God's face, he experienced a knowingness that it was God. God's voice was directed at him and said, "Get about doing what you're supposed to do... helping other people regardless of your situation. Do what I asked you to do and do it now!" God continued to talk, saying, "You've got to work with me now and don't worry about anything else. Just do what I've asked of you and do it now." Slim has never forgotten this experience, in part because it scared him. He sat straight up in his bed and knew that God was communicating with him.

Every person has many facets of themselves that comprise the whole self. Slim has always felt that he knew what God wanted him to do, even when he was struggling in his marriage that ultimately did not survive his addictive behaviors. Even when he lost his house and fractured his relationship with his middle daughter that he is now working to repair. His older daughter and son were able to forgive him and continue to bestow him with their love. He knew he had a charge to do God's work and never stop. That unspoken sense was a buoy through his life and provided him with the assurance that all things are possible. In his words, "...through it all, God's got my back!" He takes great solace in his understanding of faith and how God can love even someone like him with such an imperfect past. He knows it is his charge to remain on the faithful path to the absolute best of his ability, and to help others by providing opportunities for self-improvement through religion, physical or academic activities, or business ventures. His parents instilled in him that all you can do is provide opportunities for people; whether an individual accepts or uses the opportunity is something out of your control.

Now at age sixty-five-plus, Slim can reflect on his life and see how events in his life have prepared him for the one task that has eluded him for years. After his "dream" about God's hand lifting him, he truly began working on the project of creating a not-for-profit to serve youth. Prior to that time, he knew he could not help youth if he was still using drugs. He knew that young people would see straight through any guise he might come up with, so he had to be totally out of that world. The program Slim envisions will address the academic, cultural, and economic needs of youth, along with providing a sports outlet. He has a mission statement in mind, has worked to have the funds to support the program, and has established relationships with people interested in creating such a program. He intends to become certified as a Substance Abuse Counselor to operate the program. With the many issues youth face societally in terms of peer pressure, education, and drugs, he feels the urgent need for the program he envisions. He believes that if he "can help someone else stay away from cocaine, that will be good." Slim also has several lessons he has learned from his life experiences that he wants to share. We ended his session with Slim highlighting some of those lessons learned:

▸ When God directs you to do something, do not hesitate. Do it regardless of anything else going on in your life.

▸ Do not let anything interfere with doing God's work. Never stop!

▸ You know the intentions of your heart, so try not to let others get under your skin when they do not trust you or look down on you.

▸ Getting mad and angry is usually not productive regardless of whether you feel justified in having those feelings.

These are lessons God has imparted to Slim to strengthen him, demonstrating the never-ending faithfulness of a sovereign God.

CHAPTER 14:

Help

"God is our refuge and strength, a very present help in trouble."
(Psalms 46:1 KJV)

Pedro had to give a presentation at church in celebration of Men's Day, an annual event. The theme that year was "God's Promise." He was not even sure where to begin...what exactly did "God's Promise" mean to him or anyone else? He struggled trying to figure out what he would present to the congregation during the 11:00 a.m. service on that third Sunday in October. The harder he tried, the more stumped he became. So, finally, he decided to speak with his pastor about the theme. Pastor was always approachable, which was one of the things Pedro loved about Macedonia Baptist Church in Albany, New York. People were warm, open, and friendly, including the pastor. Pedro had been raised as a Catholic but had not practiced Catholicism in about fifty years. He was new as a Baptist...about six years. He joined Macedonia in 2013, shortly after his wife and daughter joined, and he became immersed in the fellowship. He was part of the Men's Ministry, the Audiovisual Ministry, and the Music and Arts Ministry. He felt spiritually connected to the church and its members. Joining was definitely one of the best decisions he had made in his life, but he clearly recalled the times when he had made some of the worst decisions in his life.

At age seventeen, Pedro had already been quietly "messing around" with drugs, but he had managed to graduate from Brooklyn Technical High School and follow his father's dream that he attend college. He started at the City College of New York Engineering School and was passing his classes. That was, until he met a thermodynamics course at the end of his fourth year. As hard as he tried, he could not pass the course, and he tried twice. Frustrated, he dropped out of college and moved home. Over the next couple of years, Pedro did not do "too much of anything," he says. He did odd jobs, and occasionally got high as a form of recreation. He became increasingly dissatisfied with his life, and according to the American Addiction Centers, that dissatisfaction is considered a risk factor that can lead to addiction (Editorial Staff 2019). Pedro decided to get a "real" job. He found a job as an addiction counselor. Being around the clients and in an environment where drugs were part of the culture, by 1974, he found himself using drugs more habitually. He worked as a drug addiction counselor at a methadone program and he himself was using drugs. The irony of it was not lost on Pedro.

Pedro shared a situation that occurred when he was nineteen or twenty years old living in the Bronx that could easily have resulted in his death. He set off at night in the dead of winter on one of his outings to secure drugs. He made arrangements for a pick-up at a local park at the neighborhood school. As he walked into the school yard park, he saw two guys and knew they were who he was supposed to meet. He told the guys what he had to offer for the drugs. One of the guys began to walk around him. He felt a punch in his back and began to defend himself. He was unaware that he had been stabbed. The guys seemed surprised that he had not fallen to the ground and took off running. Pedro began walking toward the street but felt heat on his back. He reached around to rub his back and found that his clothes were wet. When he withdrew his hand, it was covered with blood. It then dawned on him that he had been stabbed. He figured it best to get to a hospital as quickly as he could, so he hailed a taxicab. He told the driver what had just happened to him. The driver took him to the nearest hospital, which was only a few blocks away, and did not charge him for the ride. The hospital staff examined Pedro and were initially concerned whether a lung had been punctured or whether there was damage to other organs near where the knife had sliced into his body. No major injuries were found, but he was admitted to the hospital for overnight observation and released the following day. Pedro now says this experience was part of God's way of shaking him up – to make him pay attention to life.

During this time, Pedro would have been classified as a "functional addict," meaning he had a routine that made him appear "normal." He went to school and to work. But part of his routine was also to buy drugs to use in the evening. When he did not have money for the drugs, he would borrow it. Since he always paid the money back, people did not mind lending him the funds to support his habit. Appearances, in Pedro's case, were deceiving. Inside he felt totally out of control. Pedro was unaware that heroin addiction had become "a disease of the pubescent, adolescent, and young adults... [and that it was] the leading cause of death in New York City of those between 15 and 35 years of age...".[26] One study stated that "heroin use in Black and Puerto Rican New York City adolescents had grown

---

26 Joseph W. Spelman, M.D. 1970. "Heroin Addiction: The Epidemic of the 70's." *Archives of Environmental Health: An International Journal.*

to epidemic proportions...".[27] Pedro's path to addiction was part of a "complex interplay of multiple forces – socioeconomic, cultural, somatic, intrafamilial, psychosocial, and intrapsychic"[28] with urban poverty, racism, and easy accessibility serving as the foundation.

As he fought to maintain the face of functionality, life became more and more unbearable. He was losing everything piece by piece. His progress in school ceased because he stopped going. He lost his job, as drugs made him less and less dependable, so he was no longer gainfully employed. The most painful part, however, as his life began to spiral out of control, was that he lost the respect of his family and friends. The pit of despair for Pedro was the loss of self-respect. When he hit that pit, he awoke one morning and had a revelation that he "deserved more" and asked God to help him. With that epiphany, he began to look for a way out. In need of help, he asked his brother, who had completed a drug rehabilitation program. His brother gave him the details of a small (thirty beds), community-based program called Exodus House in East Harlem, New York. The program had worked for his brother, and his brother was back in school. In 1979, Pedro enrolled in the Exodus House program. He now believes most people in recovery realize how difficult it is to move out of addiction. As a person in recovery, it is someplace you know you do not want to be...a place where something else is controlling you.

Exodus House was run by a Methodist minister and his wife from their home. Pedro was always fascinated by the fact that the couple's two children also lived in the house. He found them to be "great kids," and their presence lifted the mood of those attending.

---

27 Jerry M. Weiner, M.D. and James H. Egan, M.D. 1973. "Heroin Addiction in the Adolescent Population." *Journal of American Academy of Child and Adolescent Psychiatry* 48-58.

28 Joseph W. Spelman 1970

The program took longer than he expected, but he stuck with it. There were specific behavioral performance levels to achieve in order to leave the program and become an outpatient where you came in periodically. As his time in the program stretched on, Pedro became restless to find a job. The program rules did not allow for clients to independently search for jobs. Typically, the program sponsors guided clients through identifying and obtaining a job. Pedro, however, took matters into his own hands and went on a job interview without obtaining permission and without making the minister and his wife aware of his intention. This breach in protocol resulted in Pedro being asked to leave the program in 1981.

In reflecting on his experience Pedro now clearly sees how the program helped him. He found another job, went back to college, and graduated with his undergraduate degree with honors. He married the love of his life (and remains married to her) and enrolled in and completed a master's degree program.

Pedro did not see a spiritual component to his long trek through drug addiction. He was just trying to get out of a place he did not want to be. He did not realize until many years later that God was saying something to him. Not until he was asked to speak to the congregation during that Men's Day service did he finally put it together. He could now articulate God's promise. To him, that promise was that God loves us regardless of how we behave and the choices we make in our lives. If one professes a belief in God, tries to live faithful to His commandments, and prays to stay in communion with Him, God will not only bless us but give us strength to withstand life's challenges.

By 2003, Pedro had completely let go of drugs, moved to Albany, New York, was married, and had adopted a baby girl. He had a good job working for the New York State Department of Corrections at Shawangunk Correctional facility about an hour and a half drive from Albany. He worked hard and was enjoying life after having survived the harshness of using drugs. It was a Friday, and Pedro was excited to head home. As he made his way to his car, he felt the chill of winter lingering in the air although spring was just around the corner. He slid into the driver's seat, fastened his seatbelt, and began the trek home. He drove the few local miles prior to arriving at the thruway entrance in New Paltz. He took the thruway ticket from the man at the booth and merged into the busy thruway traffic with commuters, commerce, and weekend traffic heading north. Pedro knew the route. It was a straight shot to Albany. About a half hour into the commute, he wanted to hear some music. He reached over to find a compact disc (CD) to put in the player. He did not realize how much this distracted him until he looked up and saw that he was uncomfortably close to an 18-wheel truck. He was in the left passing lane, so he knew there was space to the left. He jerked the steering wheel to the left to correct the situation. His impulsive maneuver put the car on the very edge of the left shoulder of the road. The car began hitting the highway mile markers. In his mind, Pedro just thought, "Oh no! My car!" He knew he needed to move to the right to get back on the road, so he turned the steering wheel to the right. At the speed he was driving, he overcompensated and moved not just into the lane closest to him but into the next lane. He had crossed two lanes! At this point, Pedro was in panic mode and tried to guide the car back into the right-hand lane, but the car began skidding toward the right. He lost control as the car skidded to the edge of the shoulder on the right and tumbled off the road.

Characteristic of New York State's topography, this section of the thruway had been built into a hilly area and the spot where Pedro's car went over the shoulder was actually above the treetops of the valley below. The car rolled over as it careened through the air. Pedro recalls still thinking what a mess this was making of his car. Unbeknownst to Pedro, the car hit two trees as it made its way to rest with him hanging upside down secured by his seatbelt. By the time Pedro's mind cleared up and he concluded that he was okay, some traffic had stopped on the thruway and a doctor and nurse had made their way to the crash site. They asked whether he was okay. He responded that he was, as he unbuckled his seatbelt, dropped down, and slid out of the driver-side window. They told him to just sit there. Someone had called 911 and in what seemed like five minutes the police and an ambulance arrived. Even though Pedro felt fine, the police insisted he go to the hospital for an evaluation.

When Pedro saw the car the following day, he was shocked to see the full extent of the damage. The front of the car was crushed all the way into the console. The car body was bent into a V-shape right in the middle of the passenger-side seat. Had the car not flipped over, that "V" would have been into the driver's seat and Pedro would not have survived. As he took in the severity of the crash, he remembered praying to God mid-air as the car was flipping over. He remembers asking that he not be taken from his newly adopted one-year-old daughter. He believes she is one of the reasons he was spared. He believes this accident was a wake-up call. It was at this point that he began to think God had other plans for him and that the accident served as a type of divine intervention. He thinks for many years he was a bit selfish only focusing on himself and what he wanted. The accident helped him to see that he was not here just for himself but for other people as well.

Pedro believes that when you go through difficult experiences it is incredibly important to look at yourself, have a little talk with yourself, and realize that you need help...and ask. He believes you must articulate the words, "I need help!" Often at such times, one is not in a position or state of mind to take those steps. If you do reach the point of making an "emotional request," as he calls it, God is there to help you. The experiences Pedro shared demonstrate that, "Amazing things happen to people and those things can change their lives."

At the writing of this book, Pedro is seventy years old and thinks coming to Macedonia Baptist Church has made him much more cognizant of what he has to be thankful for – surviving the earlier tumultuous stages of his life, surviving a major car crash, having a loving wife, and the opportunity to be a father. He now says without reservation, "Life is good!"

CHAPTER 15:

Here for a Reason

"To every thing there is a season,
and a time to every purpose under the heaven."
(Ecclesiastes 3:1)

Even now Jacq – short for Jacqueline – wonders from time to time what her purpose is and why she is here. Her life has had twists and turns and times when she thought she would not make it through the night. She has asked God many times, "Why me? Why do you continue to save me?" At times, the questions haunt her, but at age fifty-six, she has the strength to forge on regardless of external circumstances. That strength was born of turmoil, fear, determination, and surrender.

Around the age of nine, Jacq had what might be considered a life-transforming experience. However, being nine, she just considered it to be scary.

Jacq's Aunt Mabel had a friend who lived in a nice condominium and the complex had a swimming pool. Mabel was the first African American employee at Lord and Taylor in Connecticut. The job provided her with resources to access many opportunities that were atypical for African Americans at the time, such as taking yoga classes, traveling, and going tobogganing. Jacq felt excited and special spending time with her aunt. On one occasion when her aunt was attending one of the small get-togethers at the friend's condominium, her aunt told Jacq and the other children to go have fun. The adults then had space to do the same. Jacq remembers running around, playing with the other children, and splashing in the pool. As she ran after one of the other children, someone splashed water in her eyes and in the seconds it took to clear her vision, she tripped and fell into the pool. She does not remember the fall itself, but she does recall looking up through the water and seeing the light above her. The next thing she knew she was lying by the side of the pool and her aunt's friend was pumping her chest to get water out of her lungs. As one of her aunt's friends helped her sit up, the adults debated whether Jacq should immediately get back in the pool. Some said, "No, don't force her," while others adamantly expressed their belief that it would be better for her in the long run. Ultimately, the adults made her get back in the pool. That decision to this day torments Jacq and she becomes paralyzed around large bodies of water. She has tried taking swimming lessons, but that has not remedied the fear that wells up in her with the slightest splash of water on her face. However, even with the limitation, Jacq is grateful to God for not allowing her to drown.

Life continued to present Jacq with situations and circumstances to overcome. By the time Jacq completed 9th grade, the routine that had been established for her to attend a suburban school had gotten old. She was tired of using a relative's address as her home address and having to travel to that relative's house each day to be picked up by the suburban district's school bus to attend the suburban schools. Jacq told her mother she could handle going to the urban high school assigned to her family based on their address in Hartford. Her mother reluctantly agreed. During her junior year of high school, at sixteen years of age, Jacq was out drinking with friends. They were in one of the friends' cars. She sat in the back seat. The driver, a girl, was already drunk. As she sped into a gas station, her impaired ability to maneuver the car resulted in the car slamming into the gas pump. The car hit hard enough to tilt the pump to one side. Jacq's grandfather had taught her to drive when she was about ten, so she quickly crawled into the driver's seat, shoved the girl into the passenger's seat, and drove the car straight to the home of one of the girls in the car. No one was hurt, and they were too scared to report the accident. Her older sister came to take her and another of the girls home. Looking back now, Jacq knows they were wrong to hit the pump and run, but she thanks God for saving her from possibly being blown up by an explosion of the gas tank. Since the incident was not reported to the police, no one was arrested. Retrospectively, Jacq views that too as a blessing. The girls made a pact which Jacq kept, and she did not share the events of the evening with her mother, at least, not until many years later as an adult. Jacq went on to complete high school in Hartford.

Jacq was accepted at and continued her education at Connecticut State College in New Britain, Connecticut, but family issues and dynamics had their impact on her college life. Jacq met a nice guy and developed a relationship with him. Within a year, she was staying more at his place than on campus, much to her mother's chagrin. Jacq became comfortable playing the housewife. He gave her money and she did the grocery shopping, cleaning, and cooking. He also provided her with a car to commute to and from the college campus to attend classes. However, by the end of her sophomore year, Jacq was just burnt out. Trying to juggle school with the relationship and home responsibilities was just too much.

At that point, she and her then-boyfriend decided to get married. She dropped out of college at twenty-three years of age, and she almost immediately found herself expecting their first child. Her life shifted to being a wife and mother. Jacq went with the flow. She knew she needed work, so she pursued getting a job. She went on several job interviews before interviewing for a job at the Connecticut Bank and Trust. The bank hired her. The Caucasian man who hired her asked why she had dropped out of college. She replied that she got married. The man, clearly unimpressed with that response, commented, "You people don't value education." This statement stuck with Jacq for years to come, but at the time she needed to work and had to let it slide off what she referred to as her "Teflon vest" – a reference she had coined as a child to deal with any unsavory comments hurled at her. She imagined them not staying with her because, like Teflon, her mental and emotional defenses would not allow them to stick.

Jacq was good at her job of calculating the net asset value of an individual's financial portfolio of mutual funds. In fact, she was so good the bank moved her to a new position where she advised people on how to invest their money and the rules and regulations of Individual Retirement Account investments. Another year passed and, at age twenty-five, Jacq was pregnant with her second child. When it came time to deliver, she ended up needing to have a Caesarian section. During the Caesarian, she began to hemorrhage, and the doctors hurried to find the source of the bleeding, stop it, and finish the surgery. All seemed to go well post-delivery of her daughter and Jacq was released from the hospital.

Being a new mother can be exhausting with neither mother nor baby sleeping on a regular schedule. In Jacq's case, she also had a two-year-old son to care for. When her daughter was about two months old, in trying to navigate the daily demands of motherhood, Jacq found herself nursing the baby while sitting on the toilet. She did not know what was happening. She felt weak and woozy and realized she was hemorrhaging as she sat there. She tried to maintain her balance but tumbled unconscious to the floor, almost covering her baby. When she came to, she was not sure how much time had elapsed, but she was extremely weak. Getting up was not an option, so she just sat on the floor with the baby. She called out to her then-two-year-old son to bring her the phone and he did. She dialed for help. She could barely raise her voice above a whisper but told the operator where her mother worked, her apartment address, and that she had two babies with her, and the door was locked. That operator contacted her mother's job, the police department, and the property manager of her complex. All of this was good except Jacq had put the chain on the main door to the apartment. Even if the property manager came to open the door, the chain would prevent it.

From the bathroom, Jacq could hear the commotion in the hall outside her apartment door. She had lost so much blood that she could only watch and pray that her two-year-old son would be able to listen and follow the instructions being given through the locked door. The two-year-old was hesitant to do anything until he heard his grandmother's voice telling him, "It's okay, Boo." Once he felt secure that his grandmother was on the other side of the door, he followed directions to push the chair to the door, climb up, and get the chain off. No small feat for a two-year-old. Just as he had gotten off the chair and was making his way back to his mother, the property manager, the emergency medical technicians, and her mother all burst in rushing to locate her and give her medical attention. She was immediately loaded into an ambulance headed to the hospital.

At the hospital, Jacq remembers seeing a bright light and an image standing between two rows of people. She could not see the faces of those standing in the rows, but the one in the middle felt like her great-grandfather. He passed when Jacq was sixteen years old. He was the first person she experienced going through the process of dying with. He was extending his hand to her. Then she realized she was floating...just freely floating in the air. She remembers feeling like the wisps of steam as they rise from a cup of coffee or tea. She could not wait to get closer to her great-grandfather and take his hand, but suddenly she was being whisked away...moving back...darkness and coldness enveloped her. She remembers being aware that she needed to say the Lord's Prayer. She started praying, but the words were jumbled. She was floating backward in the darkness and coldness. Something told her to, "Keep saying it!" The more she prayed, the clearer and more orderly her prayer became. She kept repeating the prayer, calling the Lord's name. She felt colder as she moved backward, and then she heard a voice calling, "Mrs. Gibson... Mrs. Gibson... Mrs. Gibson!" She woke abruptly with an almost indignant, "What?" She liked where she was with her great-grandfather. She did not want to come back, and she was very annoyed at whoever was calling her. She wanted to stay "there," wherever "there" was. It was as if when she called the Lord's name she was released from the darkness. She said, "Yes!" and the nurse said, "We are so glad you're with us!"

Jacq learned that because the doctors had hurried to halt her bleeding during the birth of her daughter, afterbirth had been left inside her uterus. In a vaginal childbirth, the body naturally expels the afterbirth, but in a Caesarian section the afterbirth must be manually removed. The delivering doctor did not remove all of it. The result – the body needed to rid itself of the afterbirth and in its efforts caused Jacq to hemorrhage. Her mother told her the doctors almost lost her. Jacq would've corrected her mother to say, "I wasn't lost. I was in a better place," but thought better of it. Once again, the question she had was "Why?" "Why does God keep bringing me back?" But now she is just thankful He did bring her back.

"It's Halloween!" Jacq had driven from Albany to pick her mother up in Springfield, Massachusetts to attend a Halloween party. She was dressed as a female pirate – fishnet stockings and all. The winter of 2000 started early, and it was already snowing. She and her mother had decided they really wanted to go to this costume party, so they got in her car. Jacq had driven in bad weather before. This was the northeast; winters were always a challenge. They arrived safely and were having a good time. Jacq's sister called to let her know she needed her car keys. As it turned out, the keys were in Jacq's purse. Since Jacq had to leave, her mother decided that she was also ready to head home, as the storm had turned into a blizzard. They redonned their coats, scarves, and boots to head into the frigid cold of the night. Driving was even more treacherous than Jacq had anticipated. She inched along to get her mother home. Once there, her mother bid farewell and told her to be careful as she headed toward her sister's house. The car swerved once into the lane of oncoming traffic, but Jacq was able to guide it back into the right lane. She continued on the street she typically took but found that a tree had fallen and blocked the road. She then turned and headed down a side street. She squinted to see through the windshield as the wipers worked overtime trying to keep the window clear. She turned her defroster up. When she could clearly see, she saw that not only had another tree fallen on the side street, but that a power line was entangled in its branches. First responders were on the scene, including police, fire trucks, and an ambulance. Her mind reeled as she saw that the tree had fallen on a man. She took a deep breath, turned around, and headed for the third route to her sister's house. She continued driving at a crawl, afraid to stop for fear of getting stuck. The snow was falling faster than she could ever remember. Her wipers fought to keep pace and even with the defroster on maximum, it was a struggle to see through her windshield, but she kept moving... slowly, very slowly. CRASH! The earth shook. She was fine, but she instinctively stopped the car and looked through a clear space in the windshield. About three feet in front of her car a massive tree had just slammed to the ground. Jacq felt her heart beating quickly and loudly in her ears. She gasped, realizing that had she been driving any faster she would have been the second victim on the way to her sister's house. Hysterically, she dialed her sister's number. Her nephew answered the phone. She could not form words. They stuck and then fell from her lips incoherently. Her brother-in-law took the phone and somehow managed to get the location from her. As it turned out, Jacq was only about two blocks from her sister's house. In addition to being shaken by the power of the tree falling so close to her car, the car was now stuck. Her brother-in-law came. After she calmed down, he told her they needed to try to push the tree out of the way. When they looked more closely, they saw a power line intertwined in the tree's limbs. So much for that approach. Her brother-in-law pushed and she steered to get the car unstuck, turned around and off on yet another side road. An hour later, teetering between exhaustion and shock, Jacq stumbled into her sister's house.

The following day, Jacq learned that the man she had seen under the fallen tree had died from electrocution. The question on her lips: "Why me? Why does God keep saving me?" Her response now remains, "Thank God!"

Jacq is not certain why she is still here. She is certain of a few things at this point in her life: there is something greater than herself that she refers to as God, and God loves her. After the harrowing experience in the blizzard with the tree crashing so close to her car, when she could feel its mighty weight as it struck the ground, she has no doubt that, as her grandfather would say, she "is here for a reason not for a season." She knows that whatever the request, whatever the mission, she is willing to respond to the call. Jacq says, "Send me! Send me!" If she sees where help is needed... at home... at church...she does not hesitate. All Jacq says is, "Thank you, Lord." And "What else can I do?"

CHAPTER 16:

A Full House

"But Jesus said, suffer little children, and forbid them not,
to come unto me; for of such is the kingdom of heaven."
(Matthew 19:14 KJV)

Life goes on, as Bootsie would say. Bootsie's name is actually Delores, but no one calls her that. Reflecting over her life, she has no regrets. She was born in Catskill, New York, and has lived in the same house for almost sixty years in Coeymans, New York (minus ten years in Dover, Delaware). Bootsie is the oldest of nine children – four boys and five girls. She was also the first niece of her aunt and uncle (her mother's oldest sister and her husband), and they were beyond excited at her arrival. When her aunt and uncle came to see her for the first time in the hospital, they brought a pair of baby's booties. Delores was so small that when her aunt wiggled her feet into them, the booties appeared to engulf her whole body. Her uncle started calling her "Bootsie" and the name stuck.

Bootsie and her siblings grew up in church. Her father was a deacon and her mother played the piano. Both roles required them to frequently be at church for various activities and programs. There were Sunday services including Sunday School, morning worship service, and evening Baptist Training Union, and meetings and choir rehearsals during the week. Bootsie and her siblings had to participate in just about everything. Whenever the church doors were open, they were usually there. Fortunately, they lived just up the block from the church and were able to walk to and from church with little notice.

As in many large families, the older children often watched over the younger ones. Such was the case with Bootsie. She was charged with keeping an eye on the younger siblings when her mother had to be at a choir rehearsal, and it was not always easy. The saving grace for all of them was that most of the time she and her siblings primarily played outside. Bootsie says, "They were only in the house to eat and sleep." They played with other children in the community making up games, catching lightning bugs, and "throwing stuff" at her grandfather's pigs (for which they got in trouble). The comical part of the game-playing, Bootsie says, is that they spent an inordinate amount of time playing church and enjoying it. Bootsie was not a perfect child and would occasionally come up with an activity for all the children to participate in that would get them in big trouble. When her parents returned home, the inevitable question was, "Why'd you let them do that?" She laughs now, but at the time, whatever the response was to that question typically resulted in some type of punishment.

Bootsie did not know that her experiences watching her brothers and sisters were preparing her to play an unusual parent role later in life. She married early at twenty-two years of age and became the stepmother of two children, a thirteen-year-old daughter and an almost three-year-old son. Without the early watching over and caring for her younger siblings and the examples set by the older members of her church community, Bootsie is not certain how well she would have fulfilled the motherhood role. Bootsie had grown up under the tutelage of the older women at her church. Young girls or adolescents were not allowed to question the behavior or discipline meted out to them by the older women. Bootsie came to learn that what she and other children thought was extreme strictness or meanness was the older women's way of instilling values in their lives. The comments about appropriate clothing or demeanor received over the years taught her how to deal with criticism as an adult. It was the church community's beliefs and values that fortified her when she had doubts about her ability to parent two children before she had given birth to one. Not long after becoming a stepmother, Bootsie found herself expecting. She had a full-term pregnancy and gave birth to her first child in 1962 – a boy. The challenges of parenthood increased exponentially as Bootsie tended to the needs of a newborn while balancing the needs of the two older children and working to not show favoritism among the three. Bootsie found strength through prayer.

Over the next four years, Bootsie gave birth to two more children – a son in 1965 and a daughter in 1966. In addition, Bootsie and her husband adopted a two-year-old toddler. In 1971, her husband's sister passed, and her brother-in-law was unable to care for his three children. Bootsie, as was common in families at that time, took them in and raised them along with her children. So, at the age of thirty-three, she was the mother of nine children. She took the challenges of each day as an honor and a blessing and turned to the faith her father had instilled in her and her siblings for strength and guidance.

When asked about the faith that buoyed her through raising a family of nine children, Bootsie said that throughout her childhood her father, the deacon, demonstrated the importance of having faith in God. He likened not having faith to the Israelites wandering in the desert for forty years disobeying God because they did not believe He would get them out of Egyptian bondage and to the Promised Land (Book of Numbers – KJV). Bootsie's relationship with faith is personal. She views faith as something to hold on to, something that allows her to know nothing is impossible. With faith, she is clear that God will not allow her to fail. In looking back over her life, Bootsie is positive that it was God who guided her through raising nine children, and that her immutable faith in God will see her through whatever else life presents.

PART III:

WALK ON BY
FAITH

CHAPTER 17:

Walk on by Faith

"And Jesus said unto them, because of your unbelief: for verily I say unto you, if ye have faith as a grain of mustard seed, ye shall say unto this mountain, remove hence to yonder place; and it shall remove; and nothing shall be impossible."
(Matthew 17:20 KJV)

The faith journey continues each day as we address whatever life presents...whether we think of it as a faith journey or not. Remember, faith is basically what we believe to make life worth living. In my case, there were more physical challenges after the accident of 2002. An endocrinologist had been tracking the growth of my thyroid for a few years, but in 2013 she said it had to come out. It had grown, and although I was asymptomatic, it was no longer medically sound to allow it to remain.

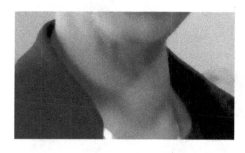

Surgery was scheduled for May 2013. The surgeon was highly recommended and skillful with his surgical instruments. The morning of the surgery, after being wheeled off for the procedure, I seemed to blink, and I was back in my hospital room with a small patch on my neck. After one overnight in the hospital, I was released to go home. By this time, I was quite the "pro" when it came to surgery. I knew all the ins and outs of hospital stays and procedures. However, my greatest peace came from knowing that this too would soon pass and that all would be well again. There was no doubt in my mind which, of course, meant there was no doubt in my spirit.

In August and September of the same year, 2013, the time had come that I could no longer put off having hip replacement surgery. The diagnosis, bilateral osteoarthritis in the hips/bilateral end stage degenerative joint disease (DJD) secondary to the old bilateral slipped capital femoral epiphysis (SCFE), had been made in 2012. However, there was no rush, as pain at that time was tolerable. The advice from the orthopedic surgeon was that I would know when I was ready, especially at the point where my sleep was compromised. By the summer of 2013, my ability to walk for extended distances was unpredictable and my yoga practice was limited, as the range of motion in the hip joints was restricted. In addition, trying to find a comfortable position to sleep in was virtually impossible. There was pain in all positions. I was ready.

Although both hips exhibited multiple bone spurs and severe lack of cartilage, the left hip would be replaced first using the anterior approach, which did not include cutting muscles and promised much faster recovery. Surgery was scheduled for August 19, 2013 for the left hip, to be followed in six weeks by replacement of the right hip on September 30, 2013. Apart from needing a blood transfusion during the surgery, I seemed to be a textbook case in that there were no surgical complications, and in six weeks I was up and ready for the second operation. Not to say that I was skipping down the street, but I was definitely mobile. The second surgery was identical to the first, requiring a blood transfusion, and the immediate recuperation followed the same pattern. However, the more extensive work of re-gaining the gait of my walk, and the strengthening of muscles to allow for greater physical activity required six additional months of physical therapy. Through it all, no pain! I was indeed blessed and thankful for my experience through these two surgeries. Miracles happen every day all around us...and sometimes to us... although we may or may not acknowledge them.

By the time of the hip replacement surgeries I was more than capable of reflecting and being retrospective about my life. Clearly, surgery, car accidents, and relationship issues were common themes throughout. Why? I like to think they were learning experiences for me. They were not fun but as I contemplate all of them, I continue to return to the thought that there is a plan greater than I can see at play. I could not allow any one situation or circumstance to define me. I could not allow any of it to determine whether I was going to have a good day or a bad day. There was always a choice to make regarding whether I held on to the elements of the situation or moved on to whatever was coming next. I chose to take whatever I could from the experience to propel me forward knowing throughout that God was – is – always with me and that my faith in Him both healed my body and my soul. Faith is a powerful force.

The faith journeys of those interviewed took them on many different paths...no two the same. Like me, many of the interviewees did not initially possess the spiritual language of faith, belief, or hope at the times they were challenged by events in their lives. In retrospect, those situations and experiences now come into clearer focus. In the following chapters, those interviewed share how they survived life experiences that led to the growth and deepening of their faith in God and in themselves. They walked on in faith.

CHAPTER 18:

Just Leave It

"Pray without ceasing."
(1 Thessalonians 5:17)

"When you leave it on the altar, you forget about it." That is Anita's belief. She left her marriage there. She left her worry and concern about her cancer there, along with fears about her daughter's survival and recuperation from a stroke. She has come through a life fraught with dangers and struggles but confidently says it is God's grace that wakes her up each day and starts her on her way. At age seventy-one, Anita does not spend her time fretting. She enjoys the time with her daughters, their husbands, and her grandchildren, along with allowing herself the luxury of indulging more frequently than she should in savory treats.

Cancer. It is a word that no one wants to hear uttered in relation to their health. When Anita heard it, she could only think of having it removed that moment, that day at least.

Her body matured at twelve or thirteen years old, and she had dense breast tissue. In the 8th grade she developed a lump on her breast that bled. At first Anita thought the spots on her bra were caused by a little rust on the bra's metal fastener. However, when she bathed, she saw the blood. She told her mother, who immediately shrieked that her baby had cancer. Her mother took her to the doctor, who thought the cyst might have developed due to Anita being hit in her breast by a ball while playing volleyball or perhaps as the result of a neighborhood boy who often beat her up. She had surgery to remove the cyst and it was sent to the lab. The report indicated that the cyst was not cancerous. She and her mother were relieved and gave thanks for the cyst not being cancerous and for Anita having the chance to live like any other teenage girl.

In 1977, when Anita was around thirty years of age, she moved to Albany from southern California, and after much searching found a gym she actually liked where she did not feel intimidated by the serious bodybuilders. She was exercising regularly but began to experience severe pain any time she attempted to do an exercise that involved chest muscles, such as push-ups. She was puzzled since the previous doctor had aspirated the cyst and found no cancer. She wondered what was causing her pain. She went back to the doctor for an evaluation. Another cyst was found in her breast. Again, she had surgery to remove the cyst, and again it was sent to the lab for testing. Again...non-cancerous. She thanked God for sparing her...again.

In 2012, Anita had her annual physical examinations by her surgeon and her ob-gyn. She was diagnosed with fibrocystic disease, which is a common, non-cancerous condition in which lumps form in the breast. The lumps can be uncomfortable and bothersome but are not typically dangerous or harmful (HealthLine Newsletter 2005-2018). However, when she went for her physical in 2013, the PRN (per diem registered nurse) noticed the lumps and thought it best to have a biopsy performed. It turned out that the previous year's diagnosis was incorrect. On Rev. Dr. Martin

L. King Jr. Day at 7:30 a.m., Anita received a call telling her she had Stage 2 cancer. The woman on the phone asked whether she had a surgeon. When she responded no, the woman gave her the contact information for three. Anita began dialing immediately. The first and second doctors' offices were not yet open. When she dialed the third doctor's office, she left a voicemail. That doctor, Dr. Valarie Brustus, accepted her case. One of her specialties was using skin- and nipple-sparing techniques during mastectomies to help preserve as much of a woman's natural breast as possible.

Anita had what is referred to as a "triple negative" cancer, which means "that the three most common types of receptors known to fuel most breast cancer growth – estrogen, progesterone, and the HER-2/neu gene – are not present in the cancer tumor. This means that the breast cancer cells have tested negative for hormone epidermal growth factor receptor 2 (HER-2), estrogen receptors (ER), and progesterone receptors (PR). Since the tumor cells lack the necessary receptors, common treatments like hormone therapy and drugs that target estrogen, progesterone, and HER-2 are ineffective".[29] In addition, the patient must be watched closely over the immediately following years to ensure no recurrence. In this case, that patient was Anita.

Dr. Brustus also asked Anita whether she had a plastic surgeon. She did not, so she asked Dr. Brustus for a recommendation... someone she worked well with...and her response was Dr. Richard AgAg. Once he agreed to work with Anita, he sought to find out how Anita wanted to approach the reconstruction process, meaning where on her body she wanted him to take fat from to create a breast. The surgery took eight hours and included the removal of three lymph nodes. Ultimately, Dr. AgAg was unable

29 National Breast Cancer Foundation, Inc. n.d. What is Triple Negative Breast Cancer? https://www.nationalbreastcancer.org/triple-negative-breast-cancer.

to harvest sufficient fat to create a proportional breast but Anita did not want to undergo a second reconstructive surgery. She would be content to use a prosthesis. The surgery was followed by four months of chemotherapy. She lost her hair, which she considers a small price to pay considering she had an exceedingly rare breast cancer.

Having a life-threatening disease changes how you perceive the world and your place in it. Anita is grateful to God and considers herself blessed to be alive. She says that it was only because of God's grace that she is still here. She believes she was spared because God had something for her to do. She has been here to care for her aunt and uncle. Her uncle had stomach cancer and lived in Alabama. His wife, her aunt who had Alzheimer's, was unable to care for him. Anita went to Alabama on September 11, 2014, to care for him. However, he died shortly thereafter on October 14, 2014. Anita thought it would be best for her aunt to return with her to the Capital Region of New York. She did, but between the cold weather and being homesick, that arrangement did not prove sustainable, and her aunt returned to Alabama.

Anita's saying, "Leave it on the altar," reflects her faith. Leave challenges and worries in your life on the altar, and once you leave them there, stop fretting about them. That belief has served her well. On April 21, 2017, one of Anita's daughters had a stroke. She was in the hospital recuperating from the stroke and had improved to the point of being moved to the rehabilitation floor. One morning upon returning from physical therapy, her daughter complained of a sore ankle, and the doctor prescribed an immediate ultrasound. While preparing to be taken for the ultrasound, her daughter suffered a pulmonary embolism (a blockage in an artery of the lungs and heart – in this case by a blood clot that had traveled from her leg) that required an emergency procedure to remove the clot. While most people would focus on the compounded health scare, Anita says it was a real blessing for her daughter to already have been at the hospital with all the necessary medical interventions close at hand (medication, medical personnel, defibrillation paddles, and other resources). Between the stroke and the pulmonary embolism, her daughter was unable to work or care for herself and her family for an extended period. And, if that was not enough, on January 10, 2019, her daughter suffered a second stroke from which she is still recovering. Anita prayed about her daughter, left that worry on the altar, and has no doubt that it was God's mercy that kept her daughter alive.

Anita continues to live each day to the fullest as she acknowledges that the cancer may come and take her away one day. Until that day, she remains, as she says, "in God's hands." Anita is convinced "the altar works!" She holds central the belief that "If you don't believe in your prayer, it's useless." She says, "You've got to believe and leave it [your challenges, worries, and concerns] at the altar."

CHAPTER 19:

Determined

"Because of his strength will I wait upon thee: for God is my defence."
(Psalms 59:9 KJV)

Although she did not realize it at the time, looking back from age sixty-two, Thelma says, "It's clear that God had a plan for me!" She says with absolute certainty that it is not just one event or experience in your life that leads you to the conclusion that "There's a God!" She is fully resolute in her belief and can tell you why and how she arrived at that point.

Thelma has always been outspoken. Perhaps it had to do with the fact that she grew up with twelve siblings and if you wanted to be heard in the house, you had to be loud and clear above the din. So, it only stands to reason that she would be firm in her understanding of where she has arrived on her spiritual journey. As for how she got there, she has had many experiences that contributed to her evolution.

As a child, Thelma looked forward to going to summer day camp. She was especially excited as the summer wore on and camp moved toward its conclusion because that is when the track and field competition was held each year. Campers were divided into east and west side teams. She was on the west. Her specialty was the long jump. There was always a great deal of excitement on the day of the competition. Campers yelled and screamed to cheer their favorite competitors on, and Thelma was one of the favorites. She recalls hearing the clamor and seeing the commotion of all the giddy boys and girls on the sidelines. When her turn came, she ran for all she was worth...and won! Thelma believes that her event win led the west team to win the competition that year. It was August 1964. She was nine years old. She did not know then that she would never run competitively again.

By November of that year, Thelma was sick. No one had a diagnosis and the doctors tried one test after another to determine just what was causing her to experience pain when she walked, be fatigued all the time, and have fevers. Her mother continued to take her to the doctor until it was decided that she needed to be hospitalized. Unlike the availability of information and resources now, in 1964 it was not known that rheumatic fever was an autoimmune disease. Rheumatic fever was difficult to diagnose. It took numerous tests and many medications to detect and treat the disease. It was known, however, that it could result in a seriously weakened heart valve. In fact, rheumatic fever was a leading cause of death in children prior to the widespread use of penicillin.[30] Thelma was ultimately diagnosed with rheumatic fever, and it did indeed leave her with a leaky heart valve.

At age fifteen, Thelma had to have a catheterization of her heart to check its condition. At that point, the doctor told her that someday she may need open-heart surgery. She emphatically responded, "I am not having surgery! I'm not letting you open up my chest!" Thelma looks back and is amazed at just how defiant she was – although at the time she did not view herself as such. She was simply stating her opinion.

---

30 David Perlstein, MD, MBA, FAAP. Rheumatic Fever (Acute Rheumatic Fever or ARF), https://www.medicinenet.com/rheumatic_fever/article.htm 2017

She is not sure of where or when the transformation started to occur. She has always believed in God, but it was not until she was a member of the Macedonia Baptist Church (Albany, New York) that she learned that God the Father, God the Son, and God the Holy Spirit are one. She is sure she was taught it, but it "hadn't manifested itself." She and the pastor (Reverend Leonard D. Comithier, Jr.) had "big conversations" in her early Bible study days because it just was not clear to her. Thelma had grown up in church and went to Sunday School, but the Holy Trinity just did not make sense prior to Macedonia. She now recognizes that her understanding of who God is and what He wants in her life is constantly evolving, and she is open to it. She admits she could not have articulated that position in her younger years.

She recalls another event that reflects the role that God has played in bringing her to this point. She became pregnant in 1976, twelve years after her bout with rheumatic fever. She had been told that she should not risk going through a pregnancy. However, since she was expecting, the doctors took an overly cautious approach and required her to be checked twice per month while normal pregnancies at the time only required a monthly checkup. The pregnancy was carried to term and she delivered a healthy baby boy in 1977. Then she was told that she should definitely not risk having a second child. In Thelma's mind, she could not see only having one child when she had grown up in a large family. She became pregnant again and again carried the child to term. She gave birth to a second child, another healthy baby boy in 1979. Looking back at this part of her life, she says without a doubt that God had a plan for her because without His intervention, her body was not likely to have survived one, let alone two, pregnancies that produced two healthy children.

Thelma doesn't think she began to fully realize how God works in one's life until she was in her forties. She had not felt well for about the first six months of 1997. She thought her fatigue and feeling "under the weather" were the result of her being "busy" with church and family activities, her job, and other demands of regular life. She did not associate any of her symptoms with heart issues. After her birthday that year, she went to the doctor because she just could not take a good deep breath. The doctor diagnosed her with pleurisy (an inflammation of the tissue lining the inner side of the chest cavity and around the lungs[31]) and gave her a prescription to get filled. Being curious, Thelma checked a medical reference about the medication she had been prescribed. The symptoms listed in the reference did not match those she had experienced and shared with the doctor. Feeling skeptical and still experiencing pain, she called her primary care physician and again shared her symptoms. Since it was the weekend, she was told to go to the emergency room if things became unbearable. She managed to make it through the weekend. Monday morning Thelma got as far as her living room couch. When her husband asked if she needed anything before he left for work, she told him that she would check with her doctor again, and reminded him that she had been told to go to the emergency room if things worsened prior to her doctor's office opening for the day. Her husband stood for a moment and then said, "Let's go to the emergency room."

Thelma spent the large part of the next week in the hospital. She started in the emergency room undergoing a variety of medical tests and procedures. As each test result came back, the doctor reported the findings to Thelma as she lay waiting and wondering

---

31 Mayo Clinic Patient Care & Health Information – Diseases & Conditions.
    https://www.mayoclinic.org/diseases-conditions/pleurisy/symptoms-causes/
    syc-20351863

what was wrong and what it was going to take for her to feel better. One test found that she had a heart murmur. She knew that. Another test indicated that she might need a heart catheterization. That was not new news either. Finally, the doctor told Thelma that she needed open-heart surgery. Although recalling that she had been told as a teenager that open-heart surgery was a future probability, Thelma was surprised that the future had arrived. Her immediate response was to surrender the whole situation to God. She trusted that God had put her in the right place at the right time and in the right doctor's hands. Thelma remained in the hospital that week to ensure the prescribed blood-thinning medication was at the appropriate dosage and working properly. Then she was released to go home for a week.

During the week before her surgery, Thelma did all the things she normally did – cook, clean, and laundry. Her husband called her job to let them know she would not be back for an undetermined amount of time. She continued to live life. When her younger sister called the day prior to surgery to ask if she was okay about undergoing the procedure, because of her strong faith, Thelma immediately responded, "Yes I am!" Even though the open-heart surgery was not something she wanted to undergo and she knew there was a possibility of not living through the surgery, Thelma was fully satisfied with her life's journey to that point and that she had had the opportunity to see her sons graduate from high school, as well as knew that they were prepared for the next phase of their journey.

Thelma wholeheartedly believes that God keeps you here until your purpose is fulfilled. She had the surgery in 1997. She distinctly recalls the anesthesiologists having trouble sedating her in preparation for the open-heart surgery. The shots were painful, although they were not supposed to be. As she was being sedated,

Thelma remembers thinking, "This could be it." That thought did not cause her fear or worry; her faith made her confident that she would have the "victory" when she woke either "on this side of glory or in the glory of heaven." When she woke up (on this side of glory), she said, "I'm still here!" That was over twenty-two years ago. Although she still is not certain just what her purpose is, she is clear that it has yet to be fulfilled.

Thelma "can't imagine her life without God or Macedonia." She views Macedonia as "a progressive, viable, and essential force" that is the "recipient of God's favor." Her perception of the church is that over the years it has continued to grow in membership and spirituality. She attributes much to the church's leadership under Pastor Leonard D. Comithier, Jr. Thelma has been a member since January 1987, and for all those years she has been under the providential care of Rev. Comithier. Over that period, she says she has grown in her faith walk and spiritual understanding. She says, "It's good if you can get there," meaning to a place in your faith journey where you not only believe in God but also know that it is the power through your faith that has brought you through each of life's challenges and difficulties. Thelma prays that everyone gets there because it is a blessed gift.

CHAPTER 20:
Death Changes You

*"Yea, though I walk through the valley of the shadow of death,
I will fear no evil; for thou art with me;
thy rod and thy staff they comfort me."*
(Psalms 23:4 KJV)

Greg's life began in the Brooklyn Jewish Hospital on October 5, 1952 at 12:30 a.m. Not many people can tell you what time they were born. The story that has been shared with him is that he almost became a Jewish baby. As is typical of many African American babies, Greg was born with reddish hair and what people call a "veil" over his face. The medical name for that "veil" is a "caul" and it is part of the mother's amniotic sac. When the baby is born, that "caul" can be around all or some part of the baby. In the early days, the "caul" was considered to be lucky and meant the child would never drown. Greg's skin was also quite fair. So fair that another lady, a Jewish lady, thought he was her baby and prepared to take him home with her. His actual mother entered the nursery just in time to prevent her from leaving with Greg. So, from the very start of his life Greg was involved in unusual experiences – before he was old enough to even be aware of them – and the experiences continued throughout his life. He shared some of those experiences.

Greg was the "baby boy." He was raised by both parents in Brooklyn along with two older brothers and one sister. A second sister was born when he was a young teen. Being the baby boy had some perks, like watching cowboy movies with his brothers or going to the park where his brother played drums and sang doo-wop with friends. Being the baby boy also had some drawbacks, like having to play with his sisters and their doll houses and newspaper paper dolls. Being the baby boy also meant, in this case, that you were picked on by your older brothers...at times teetering on the brink of being seriously injured. One brother, who was actually a half-brother with a different father, just did not care much for Greg and would try to hurt him whenever he had the opportunity, especially when he had to "watch" him when his mother was away. The brother attempted to suffocate him with a pillow on more than one occasion and once pushed him into a television, breaking the screen. He was fortunate that the splintering and broken glass did not blind him. Fortunately, Greg's mother caught on before Greg was seriously injured and sent that brother to live with relatives in the South.

Music provided the backdrop for Greg's life starting at a young age. He recalls his mother humming and singing spirituals around the house. His Aunt Viola took him and his sisters to a Baptist church, where he fell in love with the music; he remembers rocking in time with whatever song was being sung during service. Greg, his sisters, and their cousin Debra (Aunt Viola's daughter) would also listen to the latest from the Four Tops like "Sugar Pie Honey Bunch" when not in church. His brother listened to contemporary music of the time like the Flamingos ("I Only Have Eyes For You")

and the Chantels ("Maybe"). Greg remembers music filling his world whether at home or out and about. When his older brother babysat him, he would take him along to the corner where guys sat and sang doo-wop. He was mesmerized by the rich harmonies as their voices blended to create melodies that stuck with Greg. At other times, he would tag along with his older brother to the park where groups of friends, with du rags on their heads, gathered to just jam on whatever instruments were available. Greg gravitated to the bongos that his brother's friend allowed him to play. He could hear the rhythm in his head and was able to easily translate it into the notes and timing that worked with almost any song. His natural talent made his older brother a little jealous. It was the musical part of Greg's world that provided solace regardless of what else might be happening.

Greg's best friend Frederick also found great joy in music. He and Greg sang together in the school choir from 7th through 9th grades. When Frederick joined the choir, Greg knew he had found a kindred spirit. He and Frederick became fast friends. They often walked to school together and sometimes ate lunch together. Both had a quick wit and drew much attention from their peers with their antics. Greg recalls when the two of them were referred to as the "Dean Martin and Jerry Lewis" of their group with Greg being labeled as Jerry Lewis. One day in 9th grade choir during the time when Greg's voice was changing from a high soprano to lower ranges, Frederick, playing the role of master of ceremonies, introduced Greg and he was singing Ave Maria as a soprano. Other students were fascinated by the duo and encouraged them with catcalls, but a hush fell over the classroom when the teacher walked in shaking his head. No one was sure how the teacher would respond and expected the worse. The teacher surprised them all when he told Greg to continue. Frederick seemed to be able to hear the harmonies and melodies around them, just like Greg. They basked in the excitement of their voices becoming fine-tuned instruments.

Frederick and Greg lost touch after junior high school because Frederick had moved away. No one in Greg's school knew that Frederick had left high school and enlisted in the Army. His mother had signed the permission form to allow the enlistment since Frederick was only seventeen years old. He was assigned to the Infantry 82nd Airborne. Greg learned from some of his friends that Frederick was shot while on the front lines in Vietnam. Frederick's death had a profound effect on Greg. He was so deeply saddened by it that he no longer wanted to remain in the neighborhood, and no longer had a desire to "hang out" with his brother's friends. Instead he decided to enlist in the Air Force. Being under the age of eighteen, he too needed his mother's permission. He begged her to sign the papers. She did not want to see him sent to war. She asked him why he wanted to enlist so badly. Greg said it was something he felt he had to do, and that he would be able to help the family more. He contemplated which branch of the service to join and narrowed it down to the Air Force since he couldn't swim (Navy) and the Army seemed to be too close to the front line of the war all the time. His mother signed.

The Vietnam War was in the news almost every day. Greg stayed apprised of any developments in the war effort. He remembers watching all the news reels about the country's Vietnam engagement and feeling drawn to serve his country. He was appalled that his two older brothers took pride in figuring out how to escape being drafted into the military and laughed at him for volunteering to go fight. That had not dissuaded him from enlisting. He was sent to Lackland Air Force Base in

San Antonio, Texas, for basic training. In the spring of 1971, as he celebrated his completion of basic training, he received a call from his mother telling him that his brother, Ernest, who was heavily involved in the drug business, had been shot and was not expected to live. Fortunately, Greg's commanding officer without any hesitation immediately gave permission for Greg to return home to Brooklyn. He was on the next plane to New York. When he landed in New York, he went directly from the plane to the hospital where, according to his family, his brother was hanging on just to see him. During his ride to the hospital, Greg's mind was so distraught that he did not recognize where he was... the buildings...streets...his old neighborhood...nothing looked familiar.

Greg made it to the hospital in time to see his brother yet alive. When he arrived at the hospital, all those visiting his brother – family members and friends – stood back to clear the way for Greg to go straight to his brother's bedside. It seemed like seconds – maybe it was minutes – but whatever it was, it was not long enough for Greg. His brother transitioned while he held Greg's hand. Even now Greg sobs when he thinks of it.

His mind filled with questions regarding what had happened to his brother. He wanted to know who shot him. He had his ideas but wanted to know the truth. He really wanted revenge at the time. He was so angry that someone had taken the brother he loved so much away from him. His mother could see the look on his face and the intensity in his eyes and she begged him not to go after the shooter. She did not want to lose another son! Greg did not go after the shooter, but instead battled within himself about returning to Vietnam. He did not want to return and decided to be absent without leave (AWOL). That ended when Ms. Lee, a neighborhood activist who had known him for years, discovered he was AWOL, gave him a verbal beat-down, and reported him to his commanding officer. Greg was picked up at Fort Hamilton in Brooklyn, and sent to Denver, Colorado, for retraining prior to the end of his tour of duty.

Greg looks back over his life and now understands how losing people who are significant in your life changes how you view the world and how you proceed from that point. He now also understands that everything you do informs your decisions as you move through your life. When his friend, Frederick, died, Greg joined the Air Force. He is not sure he would have made that decision had his friend lived. When he lost his brother, Ernest, Greg felt as if his whole world collapsed, and perhaps it did for a while until he found his footing to move forward. Greg believes that each event in his life has helped him develop a stronger spiritual self and that without that he might yet be an unanchored person wandering aimlessly through the world.

CHAPTER 21:

Unwavering

"Hear my prayer, O Lord, give ear to my supplications:
in thy faithfulness answer me, and in thy righteousness."
(Psalms 143:1)

The woman who sits across from me is poised, articulate, well-coiffured, and confident. The story she tells reflects that her path to this point has been neither uncomplicated nor clear. It has taken her to the brink of giving up, but her faith gave her the courage to press forward. This woman, Debora, wanted to share her journey as a way to let others know that "It's not where you start or even what happens to you along the way that's important. What is important is that you persevere and never give up on yourself."

Debora was born in Newburgh, New York, which is approximately ninety miles south of Albany, where she currently lives and has lived for almost thirty years. She grew up in a home steeped with strong family ties. She remembers her grandmother and grandfather, who had ten children, with her mother being the oldest. When her grandmother passed unexpectedly in her fifties, the younger children went to live with their older siblings. Since Debora's mother was the oldest child, her younger brother, Debora's uncle, came to live with them. He was only four years older than Debora. The household then included not only Debora and her uncle, but also Debora's three siblings – one brother who was five years her senior and two sisters who were five and six years her junior – and a host of cousins, aunts, and uncles who could often be found at her house.

Debora lived in the same house from kindergarten through high school, graduating from Newburgh Free Academy in 1974. She recalls Newburgh being an "easy" place to live and grow up with a strong sense of community. There was a neighborhood corner store and the neighborhood was rich with a variety of ethnicities and cultures represented by the African American, Caribbean, Hispanic, and Caucasian families who lived there. She recalls an example of just how close knit the community was when it was time for her junior high school prom. There was a concern that the prom would only cater to the White students based on the type of music played. The principal told students at an assembly that prom was for everyone. To address the issue, the school had two bands play for prom that year – a Black band and a White band. The togetherness, however, was most evident on the dance floor when all students – Black and White – danced to every song. Newburgh was a place where "everyone knew everyone." To this day, she maintains relationships with friends from "down the block," and has even maintained a close relationship with her 6th grade teacher (and his wife), who now live in Albany.

After earning a bachelor's degree from the State University of New York-Buffalo and working for a year in a department store, Debora decided she needed to continue her education by going to graduate school. Her professor told her about a vocational rehabilitation program at New York University (NYU) that had funds available to assist students who needed them. She applied and was accepted. She graduated in two years with a master's degree in rehabilitation counseling and landed a counseling job in the Harlem office of the New York State Commission for the Blind. Life was good. She married in 1984 and her son was born in 1985.

However, things do not always go according to our plans. By the end of 1988, the marriage was failing, and the couple separated. By that time, she had been promoted to a supervisory position with the Commission for the Blind. In April of 1989, the separation was complete with Debora becoming the single parent of a three-year-old son. The family went from being a two-income family to a one-income family. Debora had been hired as a provisional appointee (a New York State Civil Service classification meaning the individual in the position must take an exam at the first opportunity and score at an acceptable level to keep the position). The state was holding an examination for her position. She had to take the examination. If she scored high enough, she would be able to keep the supervisory position and if not, she would lose it. Debora took the state examination and was shortly called for jury duty for the first time. Jury duty meant she would be out of the office for a week. Upon returning from jury duty, her supervisor called her in to discuss the results of the state exam. Debora had received the results in the mail, so she was already aware she had not scored high enough to maintain her supervisory position. Her supervisor asked her what she wanted to do...did she want to return to her former position as a counselor? She loved being a counselor and felt that was the core of who she was as a person. She enjoyed working with people and therefore did not view the situation as the end of the world. However, she did have a choice to make. She could return to her job as a counselor or work with her supervisor to create a new set of job duties.

As she contemplated the decision she needed to make, she received an envelope from Albany from the director of her agency with a note that simply read, "I thought this might interest you."

The envelope contained information about the Minority Regents' Management Fellowship Program. The New York State Education Department (NYSED) was looking for minorities to bring into the department's management positions. The information further indicated that some of the positions would be based in New York City, but most would be in Albany, the state capital. The opportunity did interest her but would mean, more than likely, she would have to relocate to Albany. That was definitely not in her plan...but neither was being a single parent.

Debora was invited for an interview for the fellowship program. When she asked about the likelihood of the fellowship position being located in New York City, the response was that the program was in its second year and its coordinator and managers wanted to have the fellows all centrally located in Albany. So much for that possibility. If she was offered a fellowship, she would have to take another reduction in pay (the first resulting from losing her supervisory position based on the results of the state examination) on top of having their family income reduced when she and her husband separated. All the while, she had to take care of a three-year-old. In addition, she would have to deal with the landlord of the apartment she leased in New York City, as well as find a place to live in Albany where she did not know anyone. Even with such daunting challenges, she told her mother that "there's a light at the end of this tunnel" and decided to go for the fellowship.

Debora says it was nothing but the grace of God that made things fall into place for her and her son. First, a friend in the city sub-let her apartment and the management company approved (highly unusual for New York City). The fellowship program coordinator introduced her to another fellow, Pat, who had been part of the program in its initial year and who shared insights, resources, and tips with Debora. This new friend took her to see possible apartments and, ultimately, she took an apartment on Church Road in Slingerlands, New York (one of many Albany subdivisions and suburbs). However, it was not available until a month after she was due to begin her position. What to do?

At the time, Debora's mother was a foster parent and cared for other children in her home. Debora asked her mother to keep her son during her first month as a fellow, and her mother agreed. For her first month on the new job in Albany, Debora worked Monday through Friday in Albany and then drove from Albany to Newburgh, about ninety miles, on Friday to spend time with her son. Generally, on Saturday she and her son drove from Newburgh to New York City, approximately seventy miles, to check on her apartment, where she still had some of her belongings, and then drove back to Newburgh. She returned to Albany on Sundays. At the end of that month, Debora was elated to move into the new apartment in Albany with her son and call it home.

The fellowship program was a year-long program with no guarantee of a position at the end. Therefore, it only made sense to take a year-long leave from her permanent position at the Commission for the Blind and to sub-let her New York City apartment for one year. What was unexpected was that six months into the fellowship program, the Office for Vocational Rehabilitation (OVR) of the State Education Department underwent a complete reorganization. The management completely changed, resulting in a new set of administrators. Six months into the program, with her background in vocational rehabilitation, she was offered a management position!

Debora settled into her position as the Manager for Consumer Services and Quality Assurance. She worked dutifully for six years knowing she again had been appointed provisionally and that the time would come when she would again need to take a state examination to keep her position. When the time came, she registered for the exam and once again found herself in a room with others seeking to either hold on to a position or be appointed to a permanent position. She felt the pressure. It was the first administration of a new state examination process, and she could not help but think about the fact that she had purchased a home and had a mortgage. She vividly recalls taking the exam and being either last or second to last to finish. She remembers putting her head down on the table and saying, "God, I've done the best I could do." With that simple supplication, Debora left the exam site and continued with her daily routines. When the envelope bearing the New York State Department of Civil Service logo arrived in the mail, she took a deep breath before opening it. Her eyes scoured the page to find her score. When Debora saw that she had scored number two in the state of all those who had taken the exam, a sense of joy and relief washed over her. Because she had passed the examination with high scores, she was appointed to her position on a permanent basis.

Debora, who retired in 2018 from the New York State Education Department as the Assistant Commissioner for Adult Career and Continuing Education Services, and now serves as a deacon at the Macedonia Baptist Church in Albany, New York, says appearances can be deceiving. No one knows anyone else's story or how they came to be who they are today. No one knows what transitions they will personally have to negotiate during their lifetime or the difficult decisions that will have to be made along the way. She has always had a belief in God and faith that things would work out, but until she had to make a way for herself and her son, she had not realized how strong she was. Now, retrospectively, she can clearly see the imprint of God's hand as He guided her along her journey. She knows that He is not finished with her yet!

CHAPTER 22:

But by God's Grace

"But unto every one of us is given grace according
to the measure of the gift of Christ."
(Ephesians 4:7)

God works in mysterious ways in our lives. It seems when we are young, we do not give much thought to anything we cannot see, touch or feel. As we mature and look back, many events and experiences become crystal clear. After being raised as a Catholic, John was baptized and became a Baptist when he was in his fifties. He now integrates his spiritual understandings in looking back over his life. He has had a lot of "firsts" in his life. First person of color to become a sergeant and a lieutenant in the New York State Police. First person of color to be promoted to the Bureau of Criminal Investigations as a Captain of the New York State Police stationed in Canandaigua, New York. First person of color to be promoted to Major and assigned as troop commander of Troop G in Loudonville, which brought him and his wife to the Capital Region of New York. All his "firsts" did not come without some angst, trepidation, and opposition. John, in retrospect, says without a doubt that he sees the hand of God not only in his "firsts" but throughout his career as he broke many racial and employment barriers for African Americans.

John was born in Salamanca, New York, a small town by today's standards, and the only city in the state of New York located on an Indian reservation. His father was a doctor and his mother a registered nurse. He only knows his father through stories his family has shared with him over the years since his father died when John was three months old. He knows his parents met while his father was in the residency part of his medical training at Homer G. Philips Hospital in St. Louis, Missouri, and his mother was training as a nurse at the same hospital. During his father's residency, his sister, John's aunt, contracted tuberculosis. John's father worked tirelessly to save her but contracted the disease himself. Ultimately, his father could not be saved and passed. His mother re-married and gave John three sisters. At the time of publication, only his "baby" sister was still living.

As Deacon John spoke about his life and what transformative faith experiences he wanted to share, he sat attentively. He portrayed the penultimate image of an officer. He sat upright, fully aware of everything around him. It was apparent that he was flipping through files in his mind...and there were many. He would contemplate for a moment and then move on until arriving at something he thought worth sharing. "Transformative" was the word that seemed to cause a moment of pause. When he did speak, he first focused on a situation where he still wonders how and why he did not die.

He relayed the following story: At twenty-seven years old, Deacon John was a young state trooper in Buffalo, New York. There had been a string of liquor store burglaries. The only description law enforcement had to go on was that the perpetrator was a "Black male." John was in the Narcotics Unit and because the case involved multiple liquor stores, the state police decided to delve into the case. The Cheektowaga police department was also investigating the case, and neither agency communicated with the other. This made for a somewhat tenuous situation. On top of those circumstances, John was assigned to the case from a handful of troopers of color in the entire state of New York at the time. As ironic as it was, a young trooper of color was looking for a "Black male." The state troopers developed a strategy to stake out a particular liquor store from the outside and were set to capture the perpetrator. Little did they know that the local Cheektowaga Police Department planned to stake out the same store from the inside.

John was dressed in a hoodie with a T-shirt and jeans in his undercover role. The Cheektowaga police thought the suspect had entered the store (which he had not) and the state troopers charged into the liquor store. Each agency's officers rushed to their assigned positions, ready to bring the case to a close. The chaos in the liquor store was deafening with men shouting, the bustling of men moving quickly, and the racket of many feet. Suddenly, John in his hoodie with his gun drawn was facing a Cheektowaga policeman with his gun drawn. John is not sure why neither of them fired as they were trained to do. In the milliseconds that passed, both men knew something was awry. Something was off. In the midst of the clamor from the other officers on the scene, both John and the Cheektowaga officer experienced a communal sixth sense. He calls that sixth sense the presence of God intervening on his behalf because if he and the Cheektowaga officer had not simultaneously experienced it, one or both of them would have been shot and injured, if not killed.

A few years later, John was at the barber shop in Buffalo for his haircut. He was off duty and just trying to relax a bit before heading back to work on Monday. As usual, the shop owner had the radio on. The regular program was interrupted to report an uprising at the Attica Correctional Facility in Attica, New York, about thirty-five miles from Buffalo. John took a deep breath. It was September 11, 1971. At the time, the inmate population at Attica was about 55% African American, 10% Puerto Rican, and 35% White. John was one of nine troopers of color in the state, and he knew his phone was going to ring. The call came. He was to report and bring a change of clothes. He and his partner, who was White, prepared to head to Attica. His partner warned him that he was probably about to witness a serious example of man's inhumanity to man. John thought deeply about that statement during the forty-five-minute drive to Attica, where they joined the growing ranks of state troopers and correctional and local police officers. When all were assembled, the count was 550 state troopers in addition to "hundreds of sheriffs, deputies, and police from neighboring counties".[32] Negotiations between the inmates and government had broken down. It had already been four days. The final proposal offered by the government had not been accepted by the inmates and the governor refused to come meet with them. The inmates held forty-two correctional officers and civilian workers hostage and had control of the maximum-security prison. On Monday morning, September 13, 1971, the New York Corrections Commissioner, with the approval of the governor, gave the signal to re-take the prison by force.[33]

---

32 *"The True Story of the Attica Prison Riot,"* Larry Getlen. New York Post, August 20, 2016. https://nypost.com/2016/08/20/the-true-story-of-the-attica-prison-riot/

33 *"Attica Prison Revolt,"* Lucien X. Lombardo. n.d. Britannica.com https://www.britannica.com/topic/Attica-prison-revolt

John had never seen or been involved in anything of this magnitude or complexity. He was in Yard D that morning dealing with some of the prison guards. He knew teargas was going to be dropped. The troopers donned their gas masks and he heard, "Jackpot 1! Jackpot 2!" Shortly thereafter, he saw the thick smoke and heard the thunder of gunfire from the rifles of troopers on the high walls around the yard. Looking back, he realizes the situation could have ended very differently for him. Visibility was extremely poor. Being the only trooper in the yard with approximately 1,300 inmates, he could have easily been hit by one of the many bullets whizzing through the air. As the confrontation came to an end, John experienced the effects of the gas and was forced to dunk his head in cold water to overcome them. "The McKay Commission, which provided the official report on the events at Attica, commented that 'with the exception of Indian massacres in the late 19th century, the state police assault which ended the four-day prison uprising was the bloodiest one-day encounter between Americans since the Civil War'" (Lombardo n.d.). Thirty-three inmates and ten correctional officers were killed during the melee. In addition, eighty-five inmates and five correctional officers were wounded (Getlen 2016). John is clear that because of his belief in Jesus Christ, God watched over him and kept him safe. He may not have been able to articulate that understanding at the time, but he has no doubt now.

Not all of Deacon John's contemplation led to memories of life and death situations. He relayed a job situation where he is sure God played His hand.

John's Superintendent came to him in 1983 with a special assignment. John was proud to have been selected, and then his Superintendent informed him he was going to Montgomery, Alabama, to help develop Alabama's corporal and sergeant examinations. John's pride turned to shock. Alabama – where the governor was still George Wallace. The same man who had blocked the integration of public schools. The same man who had allowed dogs to be used on African Americans peacefully demonstrating for their civil rights. The man he recalls standing in the door of the State University of Alabama/Tuscaloosa campus, saying, "Segregation forever." That man! John's head spun. He was not sure how he felt being assigned to assist him.

His superintendent relayed to him that as a result of a lawsuit (filed in Alabama in 1972 by the Southern Poverty Law Center challenging the segregation of the state's police system (James P. Kaetz, 2011/2017)), the state of Alabama was modifying its state trooper examinations. The state had to integrate and not only allow people of color the opportunity to enter the state trooper system, but to rise to leadership levels within that system. John could see the value in the assignment, but it took a moment to process it all.

John's first trip to Montgomery in 1983 lasted about a month. He worked diligently with the state's police division to create a corporal examination that was fair. During his second trip to Montgomery in 1984 to develop the sergeant's examination, he met then-Governor George Wallace. This trip also lasted about one month. John remained focused on the purpose of his being there: to develop examinations that would diversify the state's troopers and their leadership. At this time, Governor Wallace was serving his third term as governor, but he was wheelchair-bound since he had been shot and paralyzed in 1972 while campaigning for the Democratic presidential nomination (Britannica n.d.).[34]

---

34 *"George Wallace: American Politician."* Editors of Encyclopaedia Britannica. n.d. https://www.britannica.com/biography/George-C-Wallace

John experienced a certain level of cognitive dissonance in watching the governor serve as a very congenial, quite hospitable host. From his observations, Governor Wallace was a man who appeared to have reflected on his life and genuinely transformed himself. The governor did all he could to make John and the other two troopers from out of state feel "at home," including showing them his personal plane and assigning a State Police captain to John almost as a personal bodyguard. In fact, the captain flew the guest troopers to Mobile, Alabama, for a somewhat lavish steak dinner at a restaurant that served all White customers. As a farewell gesture, the governor held a luncheon for John and his fellow troopers. John was struck by the juxtaposition of him in Alabama having lunch with the governor who had such a hateful past. However, by the time he left Alabama, John was convinced that Governor Wallace had truly altered his view on race relations. The governor appointed John as an Honorary Lieutenant Colonel in the Alabama State Militia, and the Head of the Alabama State Police appointed him as an Honorary Alabama State Trooper.

Just as with his involvement at the Attica Prison Riot, Deacon John looks with a clearer view now. He says he was where God had wanted him to be to fulfill a specific role. At the time, he was a young state trooper doing his job, but that job had an underlying significance in laying the groundwork to integrate the Alabama State Police.

It was 1994. John was the Deputy Commissioner for the New York State Division of Criminal Justice Services in charge of the Bureau for Municipal Police. He was responsible for overseeing and coordinating the training of police officers throughout the state.

In addition, he chaired the Municipal Police Training Council and served as the governor's liaison between local police departments and the state. It was an election year and then-Governor Mario Cuomo was not re-elected to serve another term. As is common practice in New York State, in many positions aligned with political parties, when the person serving in the highest-level position is replaced, individuals working most closely to that position must resign to allow the new leader to select his or her own staff. In this situation, anyone working as a Deputy Commissioner or higher was in that circle, and that included John. He had to prepare to leave. Many around him told him he would be "safe" and not to worry. However, it turned out he was not "safe" and therefore had to prepare to find a new position.

It was just before Thanksgiving that year. He remembers coming home from church and doing something he had never done...picking up the Sunday paper and look through the want ads. Something caught his eye. An ad for a director of security for a "large upstate hospital." The ad did not indicate where the hospital was, but he decided to apply for the position. On the following Monday when he returned to work, he and his secretary updated his resume, wrote a cover letter, and mailed the application.

As John and his family went about enjoying the Thanksgiving holiday, little did he know that the director of Albany Medical Center was busy contacting his friends. However, John did not hear anything until after the first of the year – 1995 – when he received a call that Albany Medical Center wanted to interview him. It was not until that call that he knew where the "upstate hospital" was located. He went in for the interview with two vice-presidents. They commented that the interview reflected what was on his resume and that they would be back in touch. About a month later, he received a call that he needed to come in for a second round of interviews, this time with the chief nursing office, the chief financial officer, and the chief operating officer – an hour with each person.

Around the time he received the call for the second round of interviews, John and his wife planned to travel to Atlanta to visit their children and grandchildren. They set the interview up for 3:00 p.m. on a Friday just before John was scheduled to leave for Atlanta. At the conclusion of his interview with the third officer, the officer said, "If we need to talk to you, we'll be in touch!" John shared that he and his wife were leaving for Atlanta that week. John asked, "How will I know you need to talk with me?" The response from the interviewer was, "We'll find you!" John did not have a good feeling when he left the hospital. He went home and went to bed. His wife asked how the interview had gone. He said he did not know and did not want to talk about it.

The following Tuesday, he checked in with his office to see whether Albany Medical Center had called. His secretary said no, they had not. He checked again on Wednesday, and again his secretary told him no call had been received. John's wife urged him to contact the hospital himself, and after some hesitation he did. He was surprised to learn that Albany Medical Center had been trying to contact him. The woman he spoke to told him he needed to come in for a third interview with the dean of the medical college. He returned to Albany early for the interview.

Simultaneous to his job search, the state was offering an early retirement incentive. The incentive was enticing because it would not only provide a safety net for him and his family, but it also would give John the opportunity to pursue a new challenge. He decided to apply for the incentive.

A couple of days after the interview with the dean, John received a call that Albany Medical Center wanted to offer him the position of director of security. They made him an offer containing a salary figure that he just could not accept; it was too low. This was a first for him. He had to negotiate his salary. He made a counteroffer. The hospital said they would get back in touch with him after they had a chance to discuss his counteroffer. Albany Medical Center called him back that afternoon and asked how soon he could begin. He indicated that he wanted to use up some vacation and sick time prior to beginning and the hospital said that was fine. So, by Friday John had secured a new position.

The following day John had a conversation with the man sitting in for the Commissioner of the Division of Criminal Justice Services. The man said he had good news and bad news for him. The good news was that the Division of Budget had approved his application to take advantage of the early retirement incentive. The bad news was that he had to be out of his office by Friday. He laughed and asked that someone bring up some boxes so he could pack.

John is without a doubt that his experience of losing and gaining a job in a climate where his peers were fired and could not find a job anywhere was God working in his life. He believes that God intervenes if you trust Him and pray...he and his wife did a lot of praying.

Although not a job-related experience, after many years as members of one church, the pastor of that church retired and John, now a deacon, and his wife felt it was time to make a change in their lives. They were not certain of the direction their church would take but had met and felt connected with the pastor of another Albany, New York church – the Macedonia Baptist Church.

They decided to visit that church and found it to be a warm, friendly place. They decided to join. Deacon John says they are glad they did.

Deacon likes the relationships he has with people at Macedonia, as well as the relationships he witnesses between and among other people at the church. The church has numerous ministries, but he especially enjoys the Men's Ministry, the deacons, and the choir. He says, "Everyone has everyone else's back!" Upon joining Macedonia, he jumped right in to use his expertise, experiences, and skills in ways to benefit the membership of the church and the community at large. One of his first experiences involved him facilitating a safety program. He had engaged the Albany Police Department and they were coming with a multimedia presentation. He worked with the police department and had the various resources ready for the program. Then he realized he had not made arrangements to ensure that the audiovisual multimedia aspects of the program would work. He reached out to the church Audiovisual (AV) Ministry. He put the head of that ministry in contact with the presenter from the police department. Together they worked out the sound and video component of the program, and ultimately the program was a success. Deacon John was really impressed with how seamless the AV Ministry worked with him to ensure the program went smoothly. For Deacon John, some things are only clear through hindsight, but joining Macedonia was clear from the onset.

Deacon John believes that at some point in each person's life, God reveals to him or her their purpose. Some people find out earlier than others. He is clear that his purpose has been to open doors for others to move in an upward trajectory in their careers. Coming from the inner-city in Buffalo, New York, and having others in his life to lift him, admonish him when needed, and provide guidance as he walked his life's path made the difference for him. Many others he grew up with, if not dead, are incarcerated or in trouble. Deacon is steadfast in his belief that but by the grace of God he stands today.

CHAPTER 23:
Building Bridges

"And we believe and are sure that thou art that Christ,
the Son of the living God."
(John 6:69 KJV)

Angelina describes herself as a wife, mother, big sister, auntie, grandmother, and great-grandmother. She is active and busy – primarily at her church, the Macedonia Baptist Church in Albany, New York. Angelina began her life in Akron, Ohio in the 1950s. At that time, Akron was anything but a blissful, tranquil place for African Americans. Living in the city did not evoke feelings of integration or images of the cooperative, harmonious existence of Blacks and Whites. The city struggled with the same civil rights issues that plagued the nation: discrimination in employment and housing, unwarranted police brutality, and diminished educational opportunities and outcomes for African Americans.

Angelina lived in the inner city of Akron with her parents, two sisters, and two brothers. Her parents tried to maintain a well-rounded family life with church as the fulcrum between education and work. Her family attended the New Hope Baptist Church, an African American church in her neighborhood, pastored by Rev. Flynn and where her father was a deacon. Her father wanted the children to understand that everyone viewed life through different lenses and had different perspectives. He wanted Angelina and her siblings to learn how to build bridges between disparate factions, be they racial groups or other disgruntled parties. She recalls her parents' discussions about moving their membership from New Hope Baptist Church to a White church also in the neighborhood called the Disciples of Christ Church. Angelina recalls her father wanting to talk to the church's pastor, Rev. Mueller, to ensure he was aware of the actual needs of people in the neighborhood. She remembers that some people in their neighborhood did not have food or refrigerators. Although she was only eight or nine years old, she knew her father wanted to know just how this church assisted the people who actually lived in the area.

After much prayerful consideration, Angelina's parents decided to change churches and the family joined the Disciples of Christ Church. Angelina remembers that on the Sunday her family joined the church the pews were full, but on the following Sunday they were sparsely occupied. Breaking the color barrier was hard for Angelina to understand. She said, "People had to make decisions about whether to associate with me and my family." As her family continued to attend, she learned that Pastor Mueller based his actions, and those of the church, on the belief that, "We are all God's children," regardless of skin color. Although she had heard those words before, she had not experienced them in action.

Angelina's father's discussion with the pastor regarding the needs of people in the neighborhood was instrumental in the church deciding to build a center next to the church. The center included a food pantry and served as a distribution center for those in need of clothes, shoes, school supplies, and other items. Under Mueller's leadership, the church did good things for people in the neighborhood. However, there remained people in the congregation who just did not want to be around or associate with Black people

As it turns out, Angelina developed some of her closest friendships with White children from that church. In fact, they are still friends today. Those friendships resulted from her learning how to build bridges between her and children who did not look like her. During her teen years, she worked with them at the center next to the church in the food pantry to earn spending money. This early job, she believes, fuels her adult passion for working in Macedonia's backpack program that fills school children's backpacks each Friday with food so they can eat over the weekend.

Each year during her junior and senior high school years (the late 1960s/early 1970s) Angelina went to a week-long summer church camp called Camp Christian. She learned to find commonalities with individuals so they could just talk one-on-one as human beings. This approach helped her through each year's camp experiences.

Angelina, fifteen years old, with White friends at Camp Christian (circa 1970)

One year, as part of the teenage youth group from the Disciples of Christ Church, she travelled to the Appalachian region of Kentucky. Prior to that trip, neither she nor her White peers realized what true poverty looked like. They saw newspapers used as wallpaper and many children sleeping in one bed. The teenagers helped build the foundation for a new barn, but also taught the younger Appalachian children Bible stories. Angelina forged relationships with local children through showing them love.

In a different year, Angelina travelled with the church group to the Great Sioux Reservation in South Dakota near the Nebraska border to help a Native American pastor paint the exterior of the church building. That summer, Angelina learned that racial tension was not limited to those among Blacks and Whites. She observed the strained race relations between the Native Americans from the reservation and the Whites who lived in town. When she went into the town with her youth pastor and the Native American pastor, the White clerk would only deal with the White youth pastor from Ohio. She learned that neither the Native Americans nor the White townspeople were fond of Black people. Even in this environment, young Angelina managed to have a conversation or two with Native American youth around things they had in common – facing discrimination and racism and being ignored by White people.

In the 1950s and 1960s, the civil rights movement was at its height fighting racial segregation and discrimination in education, housing and jobs. Angelina recalls her father participating in one of the civil rights marches in Akron. He carried a sign that read, "I am a man!" Her father was active in the community and voiced his opinions widely regarding what he thought was injustice. In fact, he wrote editorials that were published in the local paper, *The Akron Beacon Journal,* and received insulting, often threatening, letters in response at their home such as the following one.

August 2, 1967

Charles F. Howell
599 Euclid Ave.

Mr. Howell

This is in reply to your letter in the Beacon Journal, Tuesday August 1, 1967. I have a few comments I would like to make concerning your views on the racial situation. First you negros think that the white people have no rights to any of the things they have worked, and sacrificed for all their lives. The way you people feel that everything should be given to you, it seems that your race feels that the white man owes you a living, apparently for no other reason than, that your ancerstors were brought to this country as slaves. If your ancerstors were brought to this country as slaves. If they had not of been brought here as slaves, you, and the other millions of your race would not be in this country today, which of course would be a real blessing to this nation if it wasn,t plagued with the negro race. The negro people have added very little the development of this great nation, but your race has tore down much, and is a huge financial burden to the tax payers.

Angelina remembers the Ku Klux Klan (KKK) in Akron because her father talked with her about them and showed her where they met. She remembers being surprised that her father actually had their telephone number! As in cities across America, when Rev. Dr. King was shot there were riots in Akron. Her family was one that helped make sure Rev. Mueller, pastor of the Disciples of Christ Church, and his family escaped before the fires burned down everything in the community – except the church and the food pantry/center. Her father wrote a letter to the editor appealing to the good in all to honor the memory of Dr. King.

CHAS. F. HOWELL
599 EUCLID AVE
AKRON, OH. 44307

TO THE EDITOR
AKRON BEACON JOURNAL
AKRON, OHIO 44309

TODAY, MARCH 4, 1968 THE PEOPLE OF THE WORLD AND
PARTICULARILY AMERICA LOST THROUGH VIOLENCE A MAN WHO
DEVOUTED HIS LIFE TO NON VIOLENCE, DR. MARTIN LUTHER KING
A MAN OF GOD, A GREAT SPIRITUAL AND MORAL LEADER, A MAN
WHO HAD DREAMS FOR HIM THE DREAM IS OVER, FOR THE
LIVING THE DREAMS AND HOPES OF DR. KING CONTINUE.
DURING THIS TRYING TIME WHILE THE EMOTIONS OF BLACK
PEOPLE ARE ATTEMPTING TO OVERFLOW LET US REMEBER HIS
RALLYING SONG "WE SHALL OVERCOME". LET US NOT PUT HIS
MEMORY TO SHAME ~~VIOLENCE~~ WITH VIOLENCE, RATHER LET
US PUT VIOLENCE TO SHAME IN THE MANNER OF DR. KING.
THE KILLER OF DR. KING HAS MILLIONS OF CO-DEFENDANTS FOR
EACH OF US IN OUR OWN WAY CONTRIBUTED TO WHAT AMERICA
IS TODAY, EACH OF US SHOULD RESOLVE THAT LIBERTY, EQUALITY, JUSTICE
PEACE AND THE PURSUIT OF HAPPINESS ARE NOT ONLY WORDS
BUT ACTIONS AND ARE AS NECCASARY TO FREE MEN AS
FOOD IS TO THE BODY. AGAIN I ASK EACH OF US TO NOT
PUT THE MEMORY OF DR. KING TO SHAME, WE HAVE A LONG
WAY TO TRAVEL, WE HAVE OVERCOME SOME OBSTACLES, WE
HAVE ~~ALS~~ A LONG WAY TO GO, "BUT IF IN OUR HEARTS,
WE DO NOT ~~YEILD~~ YIELD WE SHALL OVERCOME.

Charles F. Howell
599 Euclid ave
Akron, OH 44307

Young Angelina took note of her father's attempts to transcend
racial barriers and believes it fed her efforts to do the same when
in situations with other youth regardless of race. She realizes

now that her father was a bridge builder, and she takes pride and comfort in recognizing his strength and courage.

Life has presented Angelina with situations such as working with people who live in abject poverty, meeting and communicating with people from other cultures, and losing the majority of her retirement savings. In retrospect, she knows her faith in God has been instrumental in allowing her to learn to be more loving, caring, and forgiving of others and herself. She sees God as a friend, father, brother, and comforter. Angelina now shares with others that life is a journey and you have to "keep the faith." As she puts it, regardless of what life puts in your path, you "can't stay where you are! You've got to keep moving on."

CHAPTER 24:
Faith in Freefall

*"Train up a child in the way he should go;
and when he is old, he will not depart from it."*
(Proverbs 22:6)

The stories contained in this book reflect real-life events, situations, and individuals' paths to deeper faith. Many of the individuals interviewed referred to the Macedonia Baptist Church and its pastor, Reverend Leonard D. Comithier, Jr., as a source of refuge and strength through dark circumstances and difficult life experiences. Several of those interviewed indicated that they felt a kinship to the church and its members and a deep respect and admiration for its pastor. It was often that kinship and respect that initially drew them to the church and that ultimately formed the foundation for their Christian education, loyalty, and long-term memberships.

Given that common theme, as this book developed, it became clear that it would be incomplete without hearing from the man who has pastored Macedonia Baptist Church for over thirty-four years. As much as people would like to think pastors and ministers are superhumans, the truth is they are people who have also gone through, and are going through, life's challenging experiences and typically not been raised to sainthood in the process. In the case of Pastor Comithier, though, it is apparent that his faith in God is deeply rooted and began at an early age. If we refer back to the *Stages of Faith* by James Fowler, Reverend Comithier would be a person who has reached the sixth and final stage referred to as "Universalizing Faith." Fowler describes the individuals who reach this stage as having "a special grace that makes them seem more lucid, more simple, and yet somehow more fully human than the rest of us... Life is both loved and held to loosely. Such persons are ready for fellowship with persons at any of the other stages and from any other faith tradition" (Fowler, 1981, p. 201).

Reverend Comithier had no forewarning that I was going to ask him for a story. He had heard my initial request for volunteers to share transformative faith experiences two years prior but had not been involved in the book project in the interim. Sundays are incredibly busy days for pastors, with multiple services and parishioners often jockeying for position to engage in conversation. On Sunday, November 24, 2019, I took advantage of a brief window to corner him and asked whether we could schedule some time to "talk." He agreed, and we ultimately sat to talk on Tuesday, December 3, 2019.

In anticipation of interviewing the pastor, I drafted some questions which I shared with him as we sat at the conference table that Tuesday. The questions were intended to spark discussion but were not intended to place limits on what he might include in his comments. He had a couple of "hmmmms" and "ohs" as he read the questions and said he had not ever been asked to sit and reflect on his faith journey through this type of lens. He said the title "transformative" or the "ah-ha" moment can only be applied in retrospect when one can look back over one's life and gauge the impact of a particular action, experience, or event. Reverend Comithier grew up in a home steeped in faith. His father was a deacon and his mother played the piano at the Riverview Baptist Church in Coeymans, New York. Riverview was a small African American church in Coeymans, a city of less than 8,000 residents, located within a block of Comithier's childhood home. Reverend Comithier vividly remembers the many trips his parents made to and from the church to fulfill their duties and many of the conversations he had with his family and with the pastor, Rev. Samuel B. Sutton, even as a teenager. Being so deeply rooted in the church, Reverend Comithier's parents had high hopes that their son would one day become a minister. This was especially true of his father. As he grew up, "spirituality was in the now," meaning there was no need to worry about the future because their faith dictated that God would take care of it. Therefore, he did not spend a great deal of time being concerned about where his life would lead him. He knew even before he left home that everything would work out. However, this knowledge and faith did not exempt Reverend Comithier, as a young man, from having to navigate some of life's dimmer paths.

Pastor Comithier shared that after graduating from high school he attended and graduated from West Virginia State College in 1966 with a degree in education. He admitted that he was called to the ministry when he was a sophomore in college and had indicated to Rev. Sutton his intention to become a minister. However, in college, Reverend Comithier did not take action to respond to the call. In fact, he did not regularly attend church during college or in the immediate years thereafter. He, even as we spoke, could not say with absolute certainty whether it was the rebelliousness of youth or the need to exert his independence as a young man that held him from accepting his call. Whatever the cause, he knew he was not following the path God had for him. What he sees now with clarity is that events happened during the years immediately following college graduation that he believes were meant to re-awaken his faith and guide him back to the path God had chosen for him. The death of his father in 1972 was a very significant event in his life. Reverend Comithier often thinks his father died of a broken heart because his son had not pursued the ministry while in college and was not regularly attending his home church in Coeymans. Shortly after his father's death, Reverend Comithier lost his roommate, Tony, in 1973 and his grandmother in 1975. Having to walk through the pain of these losses played a key role in directing him back to the path from which he had strayed.

After college, young Leonard, with his education degree, was excited to be in a profession that allowed him to make decisions that would impact youth and eventually the world in a positive direction. He landed his first teaching position at Parsons Child and Family Services in Albany, New York. Leonard moved to an apartment in Glenmont, New York, about halfway between Albany, where he worked and Coeymans, where his family lived. He also took on a roommate, Tony. Tony was a young man whom Leonard had met several years earlier in Coeymans while Tony was in grade school and he was in high school. Tony's parents had gone through a bitter divorce, and ultimately Tony lived with his mother and was distant from his father. When Tony was younger, Leonard tried to be a role model for him, often finding time to play sports with him. Tony came to consider Leonard as a father figure.

In 1973, Tony had recently completed his military service and needed a place to live. He found Leonard and an agreement was struck. One evening, Tony and Leonard went to a poker party at a friend's place. The evening was pleasant. Nothing unusual. The party and the poker game continued late into the night. Tony wanted to make a run to the store for a pack of cigarettes, but a friend had borrowed his car. He asked Leonard whether he could use his car and Leonard agreed. When Leonard was ready to go home, Tony had not yet returned to the party with his car. However, the friend who had borrowed Tony's car had returned to the party, so Leonard drove Tony's car back to their apartment. Around 4:00 a.m. Leonard was awakened by police to learn that Tony had been in an accident in his car and killed. Leonard learned that the police had initially gone to his mother's house, thinking Tony was Leonard since Tony had been driving his car. Leonard's mother told the police where Leonard lived in Glenmont. The responsibility for telling Tony's mother that her son had been killed in a car accident was left to Leonard. Being the son of a deacon and having attended numerous funerals by this point in his life, Leonard was no stranger to death. The task of talking to Tony's mother, however, was one of the most difficult things he had ever had to do. Leonard knew Tony's mother from his experiences with Tony in his younger years. He knew Tony was an only child and that this news would be devastating to his mother. He was anxious as he approached the house. Various scenarios played through his mind. Would Tony's mother blame herself for letting Tony move out of the house when he returned from the military? Would she say if Tony had not moved out the accident would not have happened? Might his mother look at Leonard as the culprit for allowing Tony to borrow his car and blame him for Tony's death?

When Leonard told Tony's mother her son was dead and as the words penetrated her mind, she released a scream that emanated from deep within her soul. Then she just cried. As the crying ebbed, Tony's mother and Leonard sat and began sharing stories about Tony. Tony's mother talked about the struggles Tony had had with his father, and how much Leonard's relationship meant to him. Tony had shared with his mother years ago that his father came to the playground where Leonard worked to take him to a ballgame, but he did not want to go. Tony had told his mother that he wanted to stay at the playground with his friends. Leonard remembered noticing the tension between Tony and his father. When Tony asked if Leonard could go to the game with them, Leonard agreed and accompanied Tony and his father to the ballgame. Until this time, Leonard was unaware that Tony had shared that event with his mother or the significance it had played in his life. Now the memories bring him pause. At this point in his life, Reverend Comithier can see how the experience forced him to reconnect with his spiritual roots and begin to re-awaken his faith.

In retrospect, Reverend Comithier says the younger Leonard lived with a form of "faith in freefall." Young Leonard was forced to do some soul searching in the 1970s. Leonard knew, even then, that he was not doing what he should be doing...that he was off course. As a young man who had grown up in a religious home, Leonard knew he should not say no to God – as in not accepting the call to the ministry while in college. However, he figured he would get to it and was willing to accept the consequences for his disobedience to God. He continued teaching and living life until his grandmother, with whom he was especially close, died at seventy-four years old from emphysema (1975). His grandmother was the first person who told him he was to be a minister. He was eleven years old at the time. She said to him that "when God marks you, you can't get the mark off!" She watched him and nurtured young Leonard. She knew he often "played" church. In fact, when the pastor of the church, Rev. Sutton, made a house call to his grandmother's house, young Leonard told the pastor that he too had a church – referring to the barn where he would play church with other children. His grandmother took note that Leonard taught Sunday School when he was fifteen years old, and that other children and young people rallied around him wherever he went. Her death was the impetus Leonard needed to take the step to become an ordained minister. He enrolled in seminary in 1978 and was ordained as Reverend Leonard D. Comithier, Jr. in 1980.

Pastor Comithier now reflects on his faith journey. His life has been full of experiences from which he has drawn lessons to use in his spiritual growth. He likens his life in the 1970s to that of the prodigal son who, upon receiving his inheritance from his father, went off to live as he saw fit, squandering his resources along the way. When the son finally returned to his senses, realizing that he had strayed far from the life his father had envisioned for him, he decided to return home, acknowledging to his father that he had sinned against him and God, and seeking to be accepted back into the household as a servant. His father would not hear of the son as a servant and instead opened his arms to receive him with great compassion and love (Luke 15:11-32 KJV).

Reverend Comithier's faith foundation was instilled in him at a young age and resided in him even when he ignored some of its tenets. He knew without a doubt that "everything would work out." Some of the individuals whose stories you have read in this book did not have that certainty as they traversed life's terrain. However, the faith that each of them now exhibits was forged through the fires of life, and each of them, like their pastor, vow to use their experiences to help others. Based on flashes of spiritual insight, Pastor Comithier crafts his sermons by putting himself in his congregants' shoes. His messages are not merely intellectual, but an integration of his learning and his life experiences. At this point in his ministry, the gospel is like a prism that separates light going through it to allow you to see all the colors. The gospel allows him to view all of the experiences of his life and draw upon each to facilitate his and his congregants' learning.

Reverend Comithier says, "The growth of my faith was not an epiphany or one particularly magical moment but a progression through all my life experiences over the years." Growth required that he observe and reflect on the experiences he walked through, which he says is the same requirement for everyone. "Pay attention to things that happen in your life. Learn from them." He is clear that it is faith that brought him to this point, and what is faith but a belief that helps each of us make sense of our lives. In Reverend Comithier's case, that belief is unashamedly Christian.

CLOSING REFLECTIONS

Faith. It's the five-letter word that sparks much discourse and ignites the passion of legions of spiritual believers and non-believers. Faith. Something we, as humans, are hardwired to possess. Something that each person comes to define as he or she walks through life. Therefore, regardless of any religious affiliation, everyone's life is a faith walk, because we all look to put meaning to life and our experiences. We choose what we ultimately have faith or trust in – money, other people, lucky charms, government, special colors, cardinal rules of a group or organization, our personal physical abilities, or God. By the time of the 2002 accident and the subsequent surgeries, my faith was reflected in the constant undercurrent of prayers in my mind and, sometimes, aloud. At this point in my life, I am resolute that whatever the issue or situation, it is temporary and will come to an end. My vision is always on the state that I know will come and not on the temporary impediment or challenge. I have no doubt that I have been guided through this maze we call life, and that I need not worry about what happens next. I have reached the stage of faith reflected by my father's credo, "Don't worry. God will take care of it!"

As you read each of the stories in this book, did you spend a moment remembering situations in your own life where your innermost thoughts were anything but secure and you had little or no certainty that you would overcome? It seems to be the human condition to periodically look at where we have come from. The hope typically is that each of us is in a better place now than at earlier points in our lives. Sometimes this is true, but not always.

The goal for this book was not to write a sermon or take readers on a dime store journey through their lives, asking Reader's Guide types of questions to provoke thought. The hope was that as you read each story it might trigger a degree of retrospection and reflection. Retrospection. A look back to recall exactly what happened without evaluating the goodness or the badness of the experiences or events. Perhaps you took some time to consider the reasons for the situations or experiences, the outcomes, and their value. Maybe you thought about whether it was something you would do again. If so, then you actually devoted some time to reflect or look through using a more critical lens.

Every journey shared in this book is the result of reflection and retrospection. Each person's life included things they thought were good, as well as things that were not so good. It was their retrospection and reflection that brought each to share their stories with me. Each found his or her way through the entanglements of life and had come to the almost inevitable question that my doctoral advisor would pose to me at times when I thought I had reached the penultimate conclusion: "So what?" The common theme in each person's story is grace. Grace carried them through the rough places of life and brought them a sense of peace and understanding despite what had transpired. Each can now look back with clarity and articulate that it was grace that ushered them through the snarly passages of life. Grace defined as "God's unmerited favor...kindness from God that we don't deserve..."[35]

Where are you today? Now that you have grown both in age and spiritual maturity, do you have the faith – evidence of things unseen – to make it through whatever is put in your path? Is there an understanding that what is put in your path is put there

---

35 Fairchild, Mary. "What God's Grace Means to Christians: Grace is the Undeserved Love and Favor of God." Updated March 29, 2018. ThoughtCo.com

for a reason though you may not understand, BUT you know beyond the shadow of a doubt that you will prevail? Or are you still looking for "proof" or "evidence" that things will work out in your favor?

Did I know when I was a child that the surgeries would be successful? Absolutely not. BUT I had praying parents who had faith. Did Pedro or May know when they were strung out on heroin that something greater than them had a hand in bringing them through? Absolutely not, but in hindsight they can see with clarity that it was due to the grace of God that they can now tell their stories and look forward to a future with limitless possibilities.

As Min. Fullard careened off the road, did she know she was going to live through what was occurring? Absolutely not, but talk to her now. God's grace has seen many of us through all kinds of experiences...accidents, surgeries, drug use and addiction, death of loved ones...things we just could not bear alone. Where have those experiences led you? Are you still "crossing your fingers" that things will work out...or are you sure things will work out?

Everyone has a story; actually, everyone has multiple stories, and more than likely no one else knows them fully. You can be sure, though, that your assessment of that person next to you is at best incomplete. People are the composite of many things, such as their experiences, their beliefs, and their environment.

Reflection. Retrospection. Grace. Faith. Where are you?

Macedonia Baptist Church

26 Wilson Avenue
Albany, New York 12205

Macedonia Baptist Church is a faith community where men, women, boys, and girls may find God and be found of God. Macedonia addresses the needs of the whole person through its commitment to worship, preaching, teaching, outreach, and economic development. The church currently has twenty-three ministries that support the whole person, encompassing Music and Arts, Program Development and Community Empowerment, Scholarship and Christian Education, to name a few. For example, in 2016, Macedonia established the Reverend Leonard D. Comithier Jr. Institute, which provides action-oriented programs that support personal and community development and opportunities for all to access vital resources for self-empowerment.

The church is an integral part of New York's Capital Region as reflected in the programs and services it provides to the community, such as a Backpack Program that provides food to children and youth using backpacks, its partnerships with local colleges and universities to support students seeking to enter and those currently in post-secondary education, its collaboration with the local Diocese to serve as a site for a local Food Pantry, and its participation in the interfaith and secular programs in the region.

Join Macedonia for worship on Sunday mornings at 11:00 a.m. on its livestream through the church website at www.macedoniaofalbany.org, or if you are in the local area, consider joining us in person. Feel free to visit the church's website to learn more about its services and programs. If you need more information, contact the church via email at churchclerk@Macedoniaofalbany.org or by phone at (518) 489-4370.

All profits from the sale of this book will help support the programs and services of Macedonia Baptist Church.

Thank you!

EXERCISES
TO GROW YOUR FAITH

Each experience in your life takes you to a new and different "place" regardless of whether you considered that experience good or bad, meaningful or insignificant, exciting or dull. Life is a string of experiences. Some experiences we like, such as birthday parties, vacations, or graduations. Some we would rather avoid, such as paying taxes, the death of a loved one, or a serious illness. The question is what do you take or learn from each experience? How does each experience shape and guide you to move forward...or do you get stuck and remain in whatever state or condition the experience called forth from you? Who do you go to for support? Everyone needs someone some time.

Those whose stories you have read here moved past their challenging experiences, but often it was a process. They have scars – physical and emotional – but they have arrived at a place where those experiences have not left them injured, damaged, or harmed. I have numerous physical scars and evidence of surgeries and accidents, but faith in an ever-present God has allowed me to live a life beyond the healing of old wounds. I now live a life where I experience joy, peace, and happiness. How about you?

This book was written to share how its author used the situations in her life to grow and strengthen her faith. The faith journey is not tied to a specific religion or spiritual practice. If as an individual, small group, book club, part of a church Bible Study, or other group, you are interested in delving deeper into your faith journey, the following exercises may help you begin that process. Be sure to establish that your group is a "no-judgement space" prior to beginning these exercises.

Exercise 1

Every time you come through something, you make a choice regarding how to catalog and articulate your success. Some people may choose to attribute their success to their good fortune, their charisma, their intellect, their physical acumen, but you make a choice.

If you are in a group setting, each person should have a piece of paper and pen to jot notes about their responses to the following questions. Give the group five to fifteen minutes (depending on the size of the group). If you are doing the exercise alone, you may also want to write down your responses.

▸ Think about situations in your life. Select one or two to critically reflect upon.

    i. How did you survive the challenge?

    ii. What circumstances helped you come through it feeling strong? Feeling beaten up? Feeling victorious?

    iii. Did the experience change your outlook on life in a positive or negative way?

    iv. Has the experience changed how you reacted to subsequent similar or challenging situations or how you will act if presented with a similar scenario?

Allow all who are willing to share their responses – not required.

Exercise 2

▸ The author and the others in this book who shared their stories have come through many challenging situations and ultimately chose to attribute the ability to weather a storm to faith. Faith is a choice. Those in this book have chosen to have faith in God, and their faith grew over time and through different situations. Take this opportunity to reflect on what you rely on to get you through times that appear hopeless. You choose. You make a choice. Using the same process as above, respond to the following questions:

    i. What have you chosen to believe in or have faith in when you are presented with life's challenges?

    ii. How has your choice served you?

    iii. Was your choice helpful?

    iv. Did it provide comfort, peace, strength?

    v. Would you make the same choice if a similar situation presented itself? Why or why not?

Exercise 3

▸ Try a different approach to responding to the following question. If in a group, divide into subgroups (two to four people). In the subgroup, discuss the question and share responses with each other. After five to ten minutes, one person can summarize the responses for the full group.

    i. As you reflect upon your life experiences, what choices have contributed strongly to creating who you have become today?

Exercise 4

▸ Everyone in this book chose to move through their challenges and build their faith. It took faith for each person to come forward to share their life experiences with the author and with readers. However, each person trusted that their faith would see them through owning and sharing their stories. Many of the individuals found the process of sharing their stories to be very freeing or cathartic. Return to the initial process of jotting down responses to the following questions individually and, if willing, sharing responses with the full group after five to ten minutes.

  i. Do you have a process for working through significant or challenging issues in your life? If so, can you share that process?

  ii. What situations or challenges in your life, current or past, do you believe you would benefit from sharing?

  iii. Who would you share them with?

  iv. Why would you select that person(s)?

Exercise 5: Bible Study Groups

▸ You noticed that each story in the book was accompanied by a Bible verse that was selected as an anchor for that person. Now that you have responded to the questions in the exercises above, what Bible verse(s) would you select to anchor your life's journey? Why?

▸ If you are interested in further documenting or mapping out testimonies and works of God of church members, you can select which questions to use to create a larger project to show how God has worked in members' lives. Thought can be given to a creative way to display the information. Consider developing a way for members to share the responses anonymously if desired. Make this project unique to your church.

You have now taken some time to reflect upon the paths you have taken to arrive at this point in your life. You have discussed the choice(s) you have made to survive each challenge and what those choices have brought you, i.e., peace, comfort, joy, peace. You have come face to face with your faith. Before you conclude your discussions, take a few minutes to consider whether you can say you are *Scarred but Unscathed?* Whatever your answer, and remembering that faith is a choice, where do you go from here?

CPSIA information can be obtained
at www.ICGtesting.com
Printed in the USA
FSHW010938230221

9 781736 384541